Dance of the Soul

Peter Deunov's
Pan-Eu-Rhythmy, Sunbeams and Pentagram

New directions for the movements
New supporting chapters

Ardella Nathanael

∞ INFINITY
PUBLISHING

Copyright © 2012 by Ardella Nathanael

ISBN 978-0-7414-7413-1 Paperback
ISBN 978-0-7414-7414-8 eBook

Printed in the United States of America

Published July 2012

INFINITY PUBLISHING
1094 New DeHaven Street, Suite 100
West Conshohocken, PA 19428-2713
Toll-free (877) BUY BOOK
Local Phone (610) 941-9999
Fax (610) 941-9959
Info@buybooksontheweb.com
www.buybooksontheweb.com

Dedication

This book is gratefully dedicated to Beinsa Douno,
the Master-Teacher Peter Deunov, whose shining example,
boundless loving, and Divine Wisdom
has given Life, Joy, and true fulfillment
to countless souls, including myself,
and whose Light clears the way to oneness with the Divine.

Table of Contents

Maria Mitovska

Introduction by Maria Mitovska

PanEuRhythmy is a great gift from the Divine world. This beautiful circle of sacred dance opens us to the presence of Love, Peace and Harmony.

It is known that many ancient mystical schools used rhythmic exercises and circle dances as an important method for the education and spiritual development of the disciples. In these exercises Divine knowledge is hidden. It is easier for many people to accept that profound knowledge in a very simple way, as through dancing and singing.

The Master Beinsa Douno (Peter Deunov) gave the PanEuRhythmy movements and music to his disciples and blessed them to be danced consciously, with inspiration and awe. Only then may we deeply understand the profound meaning of this sacred dance and receive the full benefits from it. When we dance PanEuRhythmy correctly, positive creative energies begin to flow through us and we totally recharge ourselves. Moreover, dancing PanEuRhythmy we become transmitters of the new culture of Love, Peace, Goodness, Brotherhood and Sisterhood.

Now, at the beginning of the 21st Century, when the great transformation of human beings is occurring, a new way of social relations is more necessary than ever before. That is why it is wonderful to apply PanEuRhythmy as a perfect method for creating Harmony and Unity.

In this book, Ardella Nathanael presents the PanEuRhythmy, Sunbeams and Pentagram in a very good way, making it possible for everyone to learn the general PanEuRhythmy movements and music quickly and easily. Moreover, using her esoteric and cultural knowledge, Ardella makes a correlation with many other spiritual teachings and traditions. This helps people of every culture, religion and nation to understand and appreciate the deep symbolism of the ascending path of the human soul towards the Divine, which is hidden in the PanEu-Rhythmy, Sunbeams and Pentagram.

Coming Home

"To hear the music for the first time was to glimpse –
through the thick forest of daily life –
the well-known pathway home.
PanEuRhythmy came into my life
with the winds of the beginnings of the year
to renew in me the certainty of being able to return
to that beloved place, to the fullness of Being,
to relive the lost Paradise in the here and now.
With the first images of the dance,
the inevitable movements of the threads which direct our lives
took me back once more to the gate,
and there the adventure started again.
Each movement helped me reconnect with the Source,
each movement helped me become more conscious of myself,
of who I am and where I belong.

Each step of the dances took me to meet the Other,
that partner whom I hadn't paused to contemplate
amidst the confusion in which everyday life submerges us,
towards that Other, so remote, yet still, once revealed, so mine!
The dance helped me discover the teachings of Beinsa Duno,
and progressively astonished me
with the visionary clarity of this man
who enabled a bridge between the subtle and concrete worlds,
who through movements and melodies communicated
a teaching designed in the Heavens for present-day humanity.
The inevitable feelings of Joy and Peace –
transcending life's normal burdens –
that arise from this practice
provide the most compelling testimony
for those of us who practice around the planet.
We gain new vision on the world, on ourself and on the other,
together with greater clarity for facing our problems
and remarkable improvements in our physical,
emotional and mental well-being.
PanEuRhythmy provides a space for those
desiring to bring Love, Wisdom, Justice, Goodness and Peace
into the here and now.
It is a teaching that calls to be passed on,
a teaching that we share from our hearts,
because it completely renews our being
by filling it with the Light of the coming new times.
Since re-discovering the pathway home,
a great feeling of gratitude has arisen,
in the very depths of my spirit,
towards the Master Beinsa Duno
and towards those who, from this center of light,
spread the seeds of his teachings.
Thank you Ardella, thank you Maria Mitovska,
thank you Joro Petkov, and thank you Ramiro
for sharing with me this Paradise!"

Ana Orozco, Co-ordinating Teacher of PanEuRhythmy,
Costa Rica.

How this book came to be...

This book is truly a gift from the Divine Symphony of Life. Each of us in turn tuned in to the cosmic orchestra and found ourself playing our own unique part.

The first note was sounded on 12 August 1989, when I had a magical encounter at a PanEuRhythmy workshop in Phoenixville, Pennsylvania, with a wonderfully loving and spontaneous being, Sandy Taylor, creator of the "Rainbow Child Center." Sandy joyfully offered to follow me to another workshop and record it, which she did in Washington D.C. on 27 August, my late father's birthday.

The tune was picked up a month later, when, on my return to England, I was invited to teach PanEuRhythmy in Sheffield where I met an architect, Peter Paul Antonnelli, who urged me to write a book. When I told him it was already on tape, he arranged to have it typed for me at his own expense. During the next few months, while I continued and completed my full-time teaching job in London, and also conducted a PanEuRhythmy teacher training course, which he attended, the text was edited and mailed back and forth.

Then finally, on July 21, the day before I flew off for good to the United States, Peter Paul drove down to London with the completed book (originally called *Interpreting PanEuRhythmy*) as a farewell gift, to launch me on my new life and venture of faith. I shall never forget the sense of awe and sacred trust which this generous, unconditionally loving and gentle act of faith in me inspired, on the eve of my departure in 1990 to a foreign country without work permit or financial backing, and with only a profound sense of Divine calling.

I am still in awe at the miraculous ways in which I was guided in the following year to Terry Pezzi and Hugh and Lesley Linton, whose open hearts, vision of greater possibilities, and untiring dedication finally made it possible for me to receive a Greencard to work in the U.S. To be registered here as a "resident alien" is amusing, but perhaps not totally inappropriate, as I generally consider myself a citizen of the universe.

The cosmic orchestra crescendoed in 1996, when, through the inspiration of Jane Seligson and the loving support, tireless dedication and visionary understanding of Brett Mitchell (to whom I am eternally grateful), this book (until then only a workshop manual) was finally transformed with the help of Patricia Mitchell into a work for publication. Heartfelt thanks also go to Ken Malvino for supplying the photo for the front cover of the first edition.

My profound love and gratitude go to Maria Mitovska who has never failed in being my living link with this wonderful tradition and has lovingly, generously and wisely mentored and untiringly cared for me all through the years. Having written her own beautiful book on PanEuRhythmy, Maria has now written this very fine new Introduction to *Dance of the Soul.*

I feel a special thankfulness and warmth towards my friends, Alison and Barnaby Brown, whose enthusiasm, untiring work, and dedication to PanEuRhythmy and ever-fresh insights never ceased to inspire me anew. My heart fills with gladness as I recall how Barnaby Brown joyfully supplied the music and lyrics on which he had worked with single-minded devotion and inspiration with Vessela Nestorova, one of those closest to the Master Peter Deunov. I am also grateful to Maria Mitovska and Harry Carr, who later cooperated with Barnaby and myself to edit and modernize the lyrics in this new edition.

My heart sings as I remember Joro Petkov who worked selflessly and tirelessly with Kroum Vazharov and with Maria Mitovska, and now continues without them, to make it possible for visitors from abroad to experience the annual PanEuRhythmy camp in the Rila mountains with the minimum of inconvenience. He is a shining example of PanEuRhythmy and Peter Deunov's teachings, never ceasing to inspire us all through his Beauty-full, Joy-filled living and dancing.

My deepest thanks and heartfelt appreciation go out to each one of you, and most of all to my many inspired and inspiring teachers of PanEuRhythmy. I feel a special love and gratitude to Philip Carr-Gomm who first introduced me to PanEuRhythmy (see photo page 16,) and took me to Bulgaria in 1983 and connected me with so many wonderful people there. I am deeply indebted to Kroum Vazharov who courageously, wisely, and adroitly led the PanEuRhythmy camp in the mountains during the difficult Communist era, and personally trained me in the precision of the movements. I am particularly indebted to Leon Moscona who opened my eyes with his remarkable insights into the inner meaning of PanEuRhythmy, and gave me a rigorous and unforgettable apprentice-ship into the challenges and privilege of communicating it to others.

I have also been greatly helped and inspired in my practice and teaching of PanEuRhythmy by the books (now out of print) by Yarmila Mentzlova and David Lorimer. To the late Viola Jordanoff Bowman, the author of two inspiring books on PanEuRhythmy and the Master as she knew him in Bulgaria, I am particularly grateful for her warmth, prayers, and support.

To Phyllis Thorpe, the first person in the USA whom (to quote her own words) I "blessed to teach PanEuRhythmy" I shall always be profoundly grateful — for her deep love and whole-hearted loyalty and commitment to this work, for taking over some of my commitments when I was ill, for setting up "PanEuRhythmy: Circle of Joy" (our National Not-for-profit organization listed at the back of this book), as well as the website www.paneurhythmy.org, and for organizing a monthly conference call which links us all up in powerful ways, for her unswerving devotion to Maria Mitovska to enable her to accomplish her challenging life's mission, for her teaching of PanEuRhythmy and loving organizing of on-going groups, and for making great personal sacrifices to ensure this work continues at the highest vibration. Truly you are a spiritual daughter for me, dearest Phyllis, enabling all this work to continue on so beautifully into the future.

In the 1990's I was invited three times each to Costa Rica and Brazil. During my last visit to Costa Rica in 1998, a new and moving overture was sounded when Dora Gamboa, who had been organizing the workshops, invited Ramiro Barrantes-Reynolds to interpret, and we were at once moved by his sensitive and precise interpretation of the material. Imagine our surprise and joy when, two weeks later, he presented us with a complete translation of this book!

Then, by Divine synchronicity, on my last morning in Costa Rica, Anna Orozco, a journalist and editor who works in the Spiritual field, heard the music of the PanEuRhythmy. Anna was so moved by its Celestial sounds that she could not wait to learn the PanEuRhythmy. (see pages 8/9.) Later, with great love and dedication, she took on the task of publishing the book and making it available in the Spanish-speaking world as *La Danza del Alma.*

Now in both Brazil and Costa Rica, Paneuritmia is continuing to flourish and spread, and groups are studying the teachings of the Master Peter Deunov. These were lovingly translated into Spanish by the late Jorge Kurteff who emigrated to Argentina during World War 2, and sent them to Anna Orozco in Costa Rica shortly before his passing in 2003.

Ever since *La Danza del Alma* was published in Spanish with the new sections on the "Pentagram" and the "Sunbeams" (or "Rays of the Sun" as Viola Bowman preferred to call them), I have been wanting to share this more complete version in a new English edition of *Dance of the Soul.*

Once in the 1990's in the Rila mountain camp I serendipitously ran into a delightful family who joyfully invited me to join in their meal. Among them was Dobrinka, a radiant soul and artist of sublime spiritual quality. Dobrinka spoke only Bulgarian, but her husband was fluent in English.

Again in the Rila mountain camp in 2006, amazingly Dobrinka appeared as we gathered for PanEuRhythmy, and we danced joyfully and unforgettably together, communicating without words. Though her husband had died, her radiance still shone through her sadness.

This second edition of *Dance of the Soul* had long been held up for lack of a suitable front cover picture, though on a recent visit to Bulgaria Lilia Marinova had given me her beautiful book of poems — exquisitely illustrated by Dobrinka! One morning, while meditating on the Love of God, Dobrinka's radiance flashed into my consciousness, and I knew she was the one to ask. It proved difficult to track her down, but eventually Maria Mitovska succeeded – on Dobrinka's birthday!

In 2001 I was deeply blessed to be lovingly introduced to Sister Natacha Kolesar and visit her amazing I.D.E.A.L. community in British Columbia where the teachings of Peter Deunov and his disciple, Omraam Mikhael Aivanhov, are so beautifully lived and made available to the world. Her eldest daughter, Slavka Kolesar, is a gifted artist, so I knew at once that she was the right person to create the art-work for all the new editions (in Polish, Spanish and English) of *Dance of the Soul.* Over the next few years it was a joy and inspiration to work with her, as she gracefully and joyfully drafted and re-drafted the drawings that now illustrate this new and more complete version of *Dance of the Soul.* My heart sings and my life-blood is quickened from the ongoing fountains of Beauty, Inspiration and Joy which have poured into my Soul through the members of this loving and dedicated community.

Later, through the joyful enthusiasm of Romualda Banaszczyk (Rommy) who translated my children's book *The Butterfly Dance* into Polish, I was connected in Poland with Irena Galinska, a shining visionary and truly inspiring and loving being, who took on the great task of making PanEuRhythmy available in Polish to the people of Poland through CDs, DVDs and through publishing this book as *Taniec Duszy,* (having already published *The Butterfly Dance* for children under the title, *Taniec Motyla.)* I am profoundly grateful for the honor of meeting Irena in Poland in 2006 and the privilege of working in Poland for the next four years with her and her beautiful colleagues in this noble venture. Paneurytmia is now well established in Poland with dedicated people like Tadeusz, Arleta, Lidia and Halina continuing to teach it and organize gatherings and visits to Bulgaria, as well as connecting to people there who can help them.

In 2010 I was invited to South America to teach PanEuRhythmy in Colombia, and this was soon followed by an invitation to Chile. Since then I have been travelling to both countries twice a year, and in 2011 I published both my books in Spanish. Beatriz Schriber gave me the gift of translating into Spanish my children's book *The Butterfly Dance,* and with the loving support of South American friends and generous editorial help of Anna Orozco in Costa Rica, it was published in Colombia as *La Danza de la Mariposa.*

And now in Chile, Carmen Luz, in her loving, whole-hearted and generous way, has created a PanEuRhythmy website for the whole of the Spanish-speaking world: www.paneuritmia.com

Throughout these last two years Boris Mitov has been greatly enriching my life and work in many wonderful ways, and especially through helping me so generously with his computer and photography skills and his long experience and love of PanEuRhythmy. He has worked with me with unending patience and generosity and enthusiasm and his contributions have made all the difference in the recent productions of my books in Spanish and this book in English. My heart overflows with thankfulness for his presence and support in my life.

Finally, I want to say a huge thank-you to my dear friend, Denni, for her loving support and editing of this book, as well as to the many, many beautiful and wonderful people all over the United States, as well as in

England, Ireland, Poland, Brazil, Costa Rica, Colombia, Chile, Australia and New Zealand, who have allowed me to introduce them to PanEuRhythmy, and have opened their hearts and souls to expand my understanding of PanEuRhythmy and my own life's purpose. My heart fills with thankfulness as I remember you all and the countless ways in which you have each enriched my life and supported the work with PanEuRhythmy.

Above all, my heart overflows with joy and a deep sense of privilege and awe that my own life's pilgrimage attuned my being to the sublime music and heavenly inspiration of the work and teaching of the Master Peter Deunov, that incredibly loving, sensitive and celestially attuned conductor of the Divine Symphony of Life.

Now, with the new editions in Polish, Spanish and English, the Symphony has reached a new and moving crescendo. We are constantly renewed and transported to new levels of ecstasy by the edifying and expansive tones of the Celestial music created by the Divine Composer of the Symphony of Life

Ardella Nathanael
Spring 2012

My first experience of PanEuRhythmy, May 14, 1983

(Ardella center front, Philip Carr-Gomm beyond in a white shirt)

PanEuRhythmy – a Science for Life

*PanEuRhythmy is a Science that we can explore for a lifetime.
This is an amazing method that transforms our inner state into
greater harmony, joy and connectedness
with Nature and the Universe.
With our conscious movements we express sublime ideas
and work on our virtues and their corresponding
colors in the aura.
Paneurhythmy, the synergy of magnetism, polarity, sacred
geometry and music, is a Living Science that unveils its secrets
every time you dance.*

**Boris Mitov, Chicago 2012
(Creator of Paneurhythmy.us web site)**

My Early Experiences with PanEuRhythmy

I first encountered PanEuRhythmy in 1983, while running a meditation and personal growth group in London. I was told about a man who, in his capacity as a travel agent, was able to travel more easily in Eastern European countries which, at the time, were under the grip of Communist dictatorships and not easy to explore. This man had come across a meditative dance movement which had been taught there before the Iron Curtain, but then had been suppressed and driven underground ever since. As a travel agent he was able to move around more freely than most people, and had formed deep connections with the people who danced this PanEuRhythmy.

I heard about him and invited him to our group. We were tremendously impressed by his quality of being. Our first experience of hearing about PanEuRhythmy from Philip Carr-Gomm was like opening a door into a new world we had always dreamed of and never yet tasted.

Philip began by telling us about how he had found out about PanEuRhythmy. It was a spiritual thriller story — an odyssey of danger, daring, trust, guidance, and joy. Philip had chanced on a secondhand book entitled **The Universal White Brotherhood** (which, in modern American idiom, might be transliterated as "The Universal Fellowship of Light" or "The Community of Light Workers in all Dimensions of Being.") His search for this community led him to France and Bulgaria — the two places indicated in the book — with astonishing synchronicity.

Philip's then wife being French, they were about to vacation in France in the vicinity of the branch community led by Omraam Mikhael Aivanhov, a disciple of Peter Deunov, the adept who originated PanEuRhythmy. There he obtained contact names and addresses in Bulgaria. Then, on his return to England, the travel agency he worked for sent him as a tour-guide — to Bulgaria.

Americans may need reminding that, in the days of the Cold War and Kruschev's iron rule, travel to the Communist Eastern Block countries was fraught with difficulties and dangers. Contacting the local people could subject them to public suspicion, with possible interrogation, loss of livelihood, and even sometimes imprisonment, torture, and death.

Still, Philip risked showing one of the addresses he had been given in France to Marta, the Bulgarian woman escorting him back to the hotel in a taxi, and asking her for directions. To his alarm, her jaw dropped open and a long silence ensued. Finally she asked, "Who gave you this?"

He answered with studied casualness, "Oh, a man called Aivanhov."

Her face broke into a smile. "That's me!" she said, indicating the address.

Immediately she connected him with the mysterious inner circle of the followers of Peter Deunov, the Bulgarian teacher. This trip became the first of many, as he discovered his long-lost spiritual family and home.

Philip came to our group again (on May 14) to teach us the PanEuRhythmy he had learned in secret on those sacred mountains of Orpheus near the capital of Bulgaria, Sofia (meaning Divine Wisdom). We were entranced, and I could not rest until I had found a way of accompanying Philip on his next visit to Bulgaria.

This seemed to be the answer I had been looking for. I have always had a love of dance, but found sitting meditation very difficult. I needed something which involved my body, my emotions — everything. This is what PanEuRhythmy does. All the differing strands of my life seemed to suddenly come together in that moment and weave into a bright new picture and vision of what life could be. It was also just plain fun to do, like any dance.

I had long been interested in Eastern European countries and how people survived under the challenge of spiritual oppression. How people survive in difficult circumstances has always intrigued me, and this is also what deeply impressed me when I did travel to Bulgaria.

I met people who had been dancing PanEuRhythmy all their lives. They were so strikingly different from the other people in the country who looked gray, oppressed, and heavy, who had just been squashed all their lives. These people had an inner joy, an inner life; they knew a secret. They brought new life and inspiration to us from the West! That struck me, how people who had so much less opportunity to learn, to grow, to expand, to enjoy life on every level, could be an inspiration to me. It was so exciting!

For the first time in a decade of visits, Philip decided to risk taking a group of friends to Bulgaria that summer under the guise of a regular group of tourists visiting the sights. We were to stay three days at a hotel at the foot of the mountains and travel up in the ski lift every day, to join the PanEuRhythmy camp in the highest mountains.

The inevitable official guide was allocated to us — even though Philip knew the country well and was perfectly capable of looking after us. But it was mandatory in Communist block countries to always have a guide who would, as it were, keep tabs on us and make sure we didn't become too friendly with local people. Phillip briefed us carefully and told us to strictly avoid all mention in public of anything spiritual or pertaining to the PanEuRhythmy or Peter Deunov — taboo subjects under the repressive regime of the KGB. It was important to conceal the real reason for our visit in order to protect the Bulgarians we were meeting with. Fraternizing with people from the West was not allowed, and PanEuRhythmy was considered dangerous by the regime because Karl Marx didn't teach it. Anything that Karl Marx didn't teach was suspect in Communist countries — yoga, the church, Tai Chi, anything. Everything had to be controlled by the government. We simply don't realize in the West the extent to which everything was controlled. Teachers had every lesson drawn up for them. They had to teach exactly according to the book. The classrooms were bugged, and Marxists would be listening in to check that the teachers were teaching exactly from the book and nothing different — to the letter. Bringing color, light, and life into such an environment was a miracle in itself.

Phillip went ahead of us to make certain arrangements for us. He arranged that the Bulgarian people who were dancing PanEuRhythmy would be waiting at the top of the ski lift at a particular time on a particular day when we would just come up there. You have to appreciate that he couldn't make any phone calls or write any letters ahead of time, because all phone calls and letters were carefully screened by the secret police. So he had to travel to the country, meet the people, and make the arrangements in person, then come back and fetch us! He couldn't do it in any other way!

Finally, our time came to be in the mountains. We drove up the mountain as far as the road goes, and were then ushered into a ski hotel. It was noisy; there was loud dance music, and smoking and drinking at the bar, and so on. I felt a bit uncomfortable there, but I was looking forward, the following day, to going up the ski lift and meeting the people I had come to visit.

For me it was here that the supernatural intervened. At 5 o-clock, early on the first morning that we were due to go up the mountains, I suddenly jumped out of sleep and sat bolt upright in my bed. There was a loud man's voice which seemed to reverberate throughout the hotel, telling me that I needed to be up on those mountains; it was my business to be up there, not in the hotel. I looked around, and my room-mate was fast asleep, so I saw that this voice had not wakened her. Very quickly I realized that the voice was within me; it wasn't an external voice. I knew there was nothing else to do but obey. I packed my rucksack, while my mind sought very quickly all the implications and decided what I had to do.

This determination to be on the mountains posed obvious problems because of our guide. I didn't dare talk to Philip about it in the hotel, as our conversation might have been bugged. I didn't talk to my room-mate about it either, in case our room was bugged. Instead, I wrote a little note which just said, "Can I stay up in the mountains tonight?" I put the note in my pocket to pass to Phillip under the table at breakfast — just in case the dining room was bugged, or even the table was bugged. I knew anything like that was possible.

Phillip looked at me and raised his eyebrows. He didn't answer, and I knew why he didn't answer. He waited until we were outside the hotel on the way to the ski lift. Then he turned to me and he said, "You know, that's very dangerous."

"Yes," I replied, "but I need to do it."

He could see by the look in my eye that it was important, so he said, "Very well, then. I have already talked to the Bulgarian Communist guide, and told him that I'm very well acquainted with these mountains, and we're going to do some strenuous climbing! I let him understand that we could manage without him if he preferred to stay in the hotel. He's obviously a man who likes drinking and dancing. So it wasn't too hard to convince him. We'll ruffle up your bed and we'll make up excuses if he inquires into why you're not around with the party when we come back."

I thanked Philip warmly.

When we got to the top of the ski lift, the mountains were bathed in mist. The same Marta whom Phillip had first met very quickly took me and my rucksack to her tent, and put it away. The others went on to the place where they danced the PanEuRhythmy together. We then tried to follow them and lost our way because of the mist. So I missed the PanEuRhythmy on that first day, though we did eventually find the group.

The mist continued throughout the three days that we were up in the mountains. It was only afterwards — the following year in fact, when I went back — that the Bulgarians told us that they had been praying for protection. For them it was a very risky thing to meet us, a group of foreigners, albeit up in the mountains. Anything could have happened to them; they could have lost their jobs, been put in prison, anything. They had been praying for protection, and, as happens so often, we don't like the answers we get or don't even recognize them as answers to our prayers. We had been looking forward to dancing in the sunshine and taking photos of the breathtaking views, but we were disappointed; it was foggy and cold throughout the three days in the mountains. The fog hid the views from us, and us from the vigilant binoculars of the Bulgarian police...

It was that evening up in the mountains that the Divine purpose became clear. I was sitting by the fire, shivering in the cold mist, trying out the three languages I knew — English, French, and German — on the different Bulgarians there. One of them responded in French. I asked a question. There was a deep silence. Then the answer came from a very profound level of being, out of that deep silence. I sat up, metaphorically and physically, realizing I was in the presence of someone of extraordinary consciousness. I asked the next question with greater mindfulness. There was a deeper reflection in consciousness, and an even more profound response. As this conversation grew and deepened, I knew that was why the "voice" had told me I had to stay up in the mountains.

I knew that, if this man opened his mouth and spoke to other people in his country the way he was speaking to me, he would immediately be imprisoned, tortured, and maybe even killed. I also knew that in England I had many friends who would be deeply interested and assisted in their spiritual growth by meeting him. So it was obvious: I knew I had to invite him to England. It was a preposterous thing to do

— impossible to realize under the laws of the Communist regime, when only the aged with relatives abroad to sponsor them were allowed out of the country. Yet, there are laws and powers transcending the human, and three years later Leon Moscona came to England...

As for me, I had no idea that my whole life would be set on a new course from this time on. When I got back home, it was only to find that my husband, a minister in the Church of England, had gone off with another woman, so that was the end of my marriage. I had given up my job to work with him in the Church, so it was the end of my career. It was also the end of my home, because the home was tied to the Church and my husband's job. It was a complete breakup of everything in my life. I had built my whole life around my husband, even though I was a career woman and didn't marry until I was into my thirties. I had done the traditional, feminine thing because I had thought that was the right thing to do.

When I got back home and discovered I no longer had a husband, a home, or a job, I forgot about the invitation I had made in the mountains. But the Universe doesn't forget, and the seed had been sown... Three years later, after a series of miracles, Leon came to England. He was given unlimited sabbatical leave from his job — unheard of in a Communist country! His Father died, so his responsibilities to family ceased. Somehow, the visa was produced. My friend Phillip paid the money for his air ticket, because I was penniless at the time. However, I ended up looking after him, and a job manifested in time for me to be able to support both him and myself. For two years I fully supported him, both financially and by interpreting every conversation he had for the first six months. Finally I sent him to English classes and he began to be able to speak in English.

I took him to meet every spiritual leader we could find, and I travelled around with him. We went to Findhorn, Iona, and Glastonbury, all sacred places in England. We then went to Florence in Italy to a highly acclaimed international conference where he was invited to be the keynote speaker, with myself as his interpreter. I had a teaching job from which I could not be excused, and the conference was in the middle of term. Again a series of miracles occurred. I was told that the only way my employer could possibly give me time off — and it was unpaid leave — was if I could replace myself with a full-time teacher who would take all my classes, including my evening classes. Until two days before we left, we hadn't found anyone. Then, miracle of miracles, through a meeting at which the two of us were speaking, suddenly Grethe Hooper, a hitherto unknown person, offered. She said she did it against her better judgment; she just knew she had to do it. Grethe came to London, lived in my apartment, and taught all my classes — so I was liberated to go to this conference!

The miracles continued at the conference. We met wonderful people and danced PanEuRhythmy. Two severe financial tests occurred. I was mugged at noon in a well-to-do suburb of Florence while walking with Leon! The mugger was in a car, grabbed the handle of my bag, and drove off dragging me with him down the road, as I was still holding onto my bag (which had all my money and travelers' checks for us both.) He was so furious that I wouldn't let go that he tried to break my hand-hold against the edge of the glass of the open car window. He missed and hit his own hand instead, and so was forced to let go... The remarkable thing was that I experienced no fear throughout, and even felt a sense of compassion for this frustrated, naughty-little-boy of a man!

The second test was the cost of the whole conference undertaking. Only months before I had been surviving on welfare. Now my salary was stretched to support the two of us. I had paid for two expensive plane tickets to Italy, and we had been told the conference would be subsidized for us. We did not know we had been booked into the most expensive hotel in Florence and there were no funds to pay for that. The cost was going to put me in debt for the next three years. I prayed. On the last morning, with great trepidation, I went to ask for the bill; someone had already paid it and left the conference early! I am still moved to tears as I recall this gesture of incredible love, and marvel that I have still not learned to trust that my needs will always be met...

It was at this conference that we met Betty Rothenberger from California, who then sponsored Leon's visit to the U.S.A. That's how I came to be in California as well, and PanEuRhythmy came to be introduced in the U.S.A.

Leon's initial three-month visa lasted for two years, as the British visa offices had synchronistically been on strike! He was then invited to Ireland. This ended my apprenticeship in PanEuRhythmy, and I began receiving promptings, both outwardly and inwardly, that it was time for me to start teaching. Requests came from England and the U.S.A, and no one else could respond to them. Finally, I was invited by a community to come to the U.S.A. to teach for at least a sabbatical year.

The momentum was intensifying. How would I support myself? I was no longer young in years. How would I adapt alone in this new and vast country? If I gave up my home and job in England, what security would I have?

The first year in the USA was tough. The community didn't work out. My funds were running out. Friends were few and not to be stretched too far. I prayed for three signs confirming whether I was to stay.

The three signs were given, and I stayed. Like the widow's scant supplies, when she entertained Elijah, the funds have never run out. Friends everywhere have opened their hearts and homes to me, and unmistakable signs of Divine guidance and protection and even healing have come at unexpected moments, when most needed.

A series of miracles happened through which I was eventually awarded a Greencard. For eight years I was without any real home, staying in other people's homes while travelling and teaching PanEuRhythmy almost continuously around the continents of North, South and Central America. I also made trips to England, Bulgaria, Ireland, Australia and New Zealand. I met wonderful people and was somehow always protected, though the stress at times was intense.

Through the amazing odyssey of adventures that make up my life, I am never allowed to become complacent — or bored! In my wildest dreams I would never have visualized all the adventures, excitement, encounters, opportunities, challenges, fears, personal growth, pain, and, above all, the joy and fulfillment that have come my way through teaching PanEuRhythmy.

My heart is full as I remember all the opportunities to live by faith and learn and grow, and how even the most painful, threatening experiences turn to joy and expansion of consciousness, when embraced with thankfulness.

My Experience of Dancing the Paneurhythmy

It is a wonderful thing to dance the Paneurhythmy
in a circle of fellow spiritual aspirants.
The air is gentle upon our faces, the turf soft beneath our feet
and the music is of another world - the Divine.
Put this circle of dancers, dressed in white, in the Rila mountains
in Bulgaria, in a setting close to one of the seven sacred lakes,
and hear the compelling strains of the holy music,
pouring forth from the musicians in the centre of the circle,
and you will begin to get a picture of what it is like
to dance the Paneurhythmy in its native setting.

But wherever you dance it, the great angels who guide this work
will sweep down and enfold all the dancers in their divine love,
and hills and meadows and rivers will rejoice,
and dancers and devas and the world of nature will become one
in the healing love of the Divine.

I first danced the Paneurhythmy in Iona, Scotland.
We were given a field by a local farmer, and we got up early
to perform it before the cows returned from milking.
It was a rough field, full of lumps and cow pat and nettles,
and we wore our walking boots, and we were not in white.
Nevertheless, after our first practice steps
and a little understanding of what to do with our feet and arms,
we soon began to sense the power of this dance,
how perfectly it has been created to draw the dancers,
the world of nature and the great beings of the landscape
into a profound and beautiful harmony.
Then I was shown a picture of the Master Peter Deunov
who gave this dance in the last century,
and I have never looked back since.
I have danced it regularly, and several times I have had
the great privilege of dancing it in the sacred Rila mountains.
It has brought me a further step along my Path,
nay, a great stride!

Morelle Forster, England and USA

Introducing Peter Deunov's PanEuRhythmy

I would like to briefly define what the word PanEuRhythmy means. **Pan**, in Greek, means "all-over," (as in Pan-African, Pan-American, and so on,) therefore Nature, Universe, the whole of Creation; **Eu** means good or harmonious; and **Rhythmy** means rhythmic movement. So **Pan-Eu-Rhythmy** means "the rhythm and harmony of the Universe." PanEuRhythmy is a dance-exercise-meditation which can enable us to attune to the rhythm and harmony of the universe. ***

The secret power of PanEuRhythmy is in its music. I know of no other great Spiritual Master than Peter Deunov who was also a composer of sublimely inspiring music which can awaken the Soul in a powerful way. Peter Deunov himself said that he simply gave physical expression to music he could hear in the Divine world.

*** For the **Seven Principles underlying PanEuRhythmy**, (which need deeper study than is possible here,) see www.paneurhythmy.us About PanEuRhythmy

Two people I know have "remembered" this music from before they were born or from a Near Death Experience. Countless others have been transformed or healed by this music.

The PanEuRhythmy consists of a series of 28 "movements." Each movement of the PanEuRhythmy expresses something of the inner meaning of its music, and in this way amplifies our ability to benefit from it — as long as we pay real attention to the music and allow the music to express itself through our mind, feelings and bodily motion. Peter Deunov himself said that the movements alone would just be another form of physical exercise, and are not the true PanEuRhythmy.

PanEuRhythmy enhances our abilities to cope with the challenges of life at this time of expansion into global and universal consciousness. It was created to enable us to expand our consciousness and open up our understanding, our hearts, and our physical, mental, and spiritual levels of being, so that we can attune to the increase in awareness, the speeding up of vibration, and the acceleration of events and evolution that are going on at the moment. As Isadora Duncan said, there is a great new upsurge of consciousness and quest for the ultimate dance of creation, just now. Mankind is at a crossroads. We could make a whole new evolutionary leap to a new level of consciousness, or we could extinguish life on this planet altogether. PanEuRhythmy was created precisely for this day and age, for people of all ages and all walks of life the world over.

PanEuRhythmy has qualities in common with Yoga, Tai Chi and Chi Gung in that each movement acts on higher energy centers and opens up our consciousness. Through the music and the movements together it works on the heart and on the whole body and nervous system. It is intended to be a daily morning practice to set the tone for the day.

PanEuRhythmy can become a personal meditation with profound inner meaning. Each movement is like a Japanese "koan." Peter Dawkins, a leading spiritual teacher in England, incorporates PanEuRhythmy into his conferences because it "enables people to attain deeper insights and understanding than they would otherwise obtain," and said of the PanEuRhythmy that its inner meaning is something that it would take a lifetime to deepen and understand.

PanEuRhythmy helps us to get out of the chatter of our minds, and to appreciate the true workings and functioning of Mind. One of the movements called **Think!** shows us how the true use of Mind is to be silently receptive to Higher, Universal Mind, to capture those great thoughts which are waiting for our consciousness to be ready to receive them, and then to work with them to evolve *"Something Beautiful for God,"* to quote from Mother Teresa.

Whenever one dances the PanEuRhythmy with others, it is as if a link, a deep bond, is created with those people. When one sees them again, it is like recognizing family — spiritual family. People from totally different backgrounds can dance together, and, though they may not know one another to start with, by the end they feel they belong together.

How is it done? I can only say that the music, the movements and the attunement to Nature have to be experienced. Dancing outdoors in Nature is another important part of PanEuRhythmy. It can be danced indoors, but there is an element missing. It needs to be done preferably early in the morning, out of doors. Generally, when we dance, the sun comes out, we connect with Nature and even the animals and birds join in. Clairvoyant people say that the little folk, the fairies, the elves, the tree devas, also join in. One such person once reported how the flower fairies left their flowers and came and danced in the center of our circle, because they were so happy to see human beings dancing a dance similar to their own.

PanEuRhythmy is a dance that links us with the angelic world, attuning us to the true essence of life, to that which is most profound, highest, greatest, and universal. In doing so, all our faculties open. We discover our interconnectedness in universal oneness.

PanEuRhythmy was given to humanity through the Master Peter Deunov to help us make this great evolutionary leap into the next millennium. PanEuRhythmy is a modern dance, but it is also very ancient, in that it is archetypal. The archetypes of PanEuRhythmy take us right back to the ancient sources of sacred dance, and they bring back the meanings and significance that have been lost in many other forms of sacred dance.

A great and prolific esoteric musician, Peter Deunov told of how different kinds of music work on different levels of our being: some music activates the physical level of our being, other music opens the heart, and esoteric or spiritual music enables the expression of the soul and spirit. The PanEuRhythmy music works on our whole being, but particularly on our higher energy centers.

The music for each dance actually produces its own unique movement. This is borne out by the experience of many. A brave teacher in the Soviet Union once wanted to share the PanEuRhythmy with her five-year-old pupils, but normally it was totally impossible to teach anything other than the assigned lesson prescribed for every day of the week by a central authority. Throughout the Soviet Union all teachers would be teaching exactly the same lesson to a particular age group, and the classrooms were bugged to ensure that the teacher was keeping to the letter of the lesson. Of course, there was no freedom of access to books from the West; only Marxist-produced or approved books were available. It was like living in a straight jacket, mentally. However, this teacher finally found the opportunity she was looking for — a lesson of free movement to music. So she told the children, "Today I'm just going to play music, and I want you to dance around any way you like to this music," and she played the music of the PanEuRhythmy as if she was just extemporizing. As she played and watched the children, she found to her astonishment that they were dancing the movements of the PanEuRhythmy...

When Yarmila Mentzlova, a student of Isadora Duncan, came to see Peter Deunov and first heard the PanEuRhythmy music, she danced the movements without ever having been taught them. Peter Deunov then pointed out to the people around that, for those who have ears to hear, the movements arise naturally out of the music. Later he asked her to write a comprehensive book on PanEuRhythmy, (which she did in French, now out of print.) Her descriptions of the movements of PanEuRhythmy are so accurate and precise that they have always been regarded as the standard, and they certainly were to me as I learnt and re-learnt and taught these beautiful movements over the years.

PanEuRhythmy brings great benefits to all who practice it. I remember a woman who was very overweight and ungainly, dancing with great difficulty. Afterwards I learned that she had broken her Achilles tendon and had not been able to walk for three months. She was just beginning to walk again and was determined to learn the PanEuRhythmy. When I returned to her area a month later, she was walking like a queen, with real grace and elegance. Although she was still overweight, she looked majestic instead of ungainly as she had on the previous occasion. Everyone in the workshop noticed and, when we commented, she said, "I've been dancing PanEuRhythmy every day since our last workshop, in my garden early in the morning. It's made all the difference." She then added, "Until now, I was so ashamed of my body that I used to act as if I didn't have a body. Now I feel proud and good about my body and feel a sense of grace flowing through me." She continued, "My leg has now mended, and I'm walking equally easily with both legs."

PanEuRhythmy loosens up one's limbs. I personally used to have arthritis and it's helped me enormously. Other people have also found that it helps with arthritis and many other ailments.

PanEuRhythmy has also opened up my mind and my consciousness. Every time I dance it, it's as if I were going up in a helicopter or a balloon from my everyday life. I'm no longer seeing just that section of the road I'm traveling on. I'm seeing the bigger picture and how different parts of my life tie in together. If I wake up feeling depressed or down, the depression lifts and there's a new joy that comes in.

Many other people have testified to this, and I can see this is the secret of that joy that I experienced in those people who were under Communist oppression. It gives one that connection with meaning, with purpose, with the Whole which often eludes us in the humdrum course of our lives, so we need to reconnect each morning if we are going to live our day fully and meaningfully. It's like switching on the light and no longer walking in the dark. Life suddenly becomes meaningful, colorful, bright, and alive.

Essentially we know that we are one with all life, and yet somehow our everyday experience is that we are fragmented. So we seek various practices to reconnect with ourselves — philosophy, movement, therapies, working through emotional releases, going to workshops, meeting friends, marriage, falling in love, all differing ways of discovering oneness. Yet this essential oneness is there all the time, and PanEuRhythmy is a beautiful way of rediscovering it.

PanEuRhythmy, being both ancient and modern, was given very consciously to help us penetrate to the inner significance and meaning and understanding of life and our Divine purpose. PanEuRhythmy helps us enter into and experience the symphony of creation, allegorically expressed in the ancient tradition of India in the dance of Shiva.

To quote from Peter Deunov himself:

"PanEuRhythmy is the method which can help man
restore his relationship with nature...
employing air as the most modern, most effective,
and fastest way of intercommunication...
with the world and Nature...

"Music is the language of the Spirit...
The harmony of the spheres is a reality...
The whole universe is singing;
the sea, the earth, the whole starry system...

"To develop a musical nature,
you must focus your attention on spiritual values,
for in the Spiritual dimension
all energy and every living form finds its expression
through the fundamental laws of music...

"There is music in running water,
in the blowing of wind, in the rustling of leaves,
and in the singing of birds...

When man develops his cosmic consciousness,
he will become aware of the great symphony
which can be heard throughout the universe.

Only then will he understand the profound meaning of life."

As in all the spiritual traditions of the world, in the beginning of St. John's Gospel we read, **"In the beginning was the Word, and the Word was with God and the Word was God."** That is a very rough translation of the Greek, which actually means, **"In the beginning God expressed himself, by uttering a musical sound, and that sound was creative. It was that sound that gave rise to all that is in the Universe."** Now this may seem far-fetched, but scientists nowadays are discovering its truth.

31

If you put a tuning-fork on a sand-tray or on water, every different note creates a different pattern. We also know that different music has different effects on us. In Dr Emoto's DVD, *Messages from Water* one can literally watch water crystals growing beautiful palm-fronds under the influence of beautiful music, the quality and shape of the fronds at all times expressing and reflecting the quality of the particular music being played.

Stephen Halpern and other musicians, both East and West, have also been researching the effects of different forms of music on the body, psyche, brain, and spirit, not only of human beings, but also of animals and plants. This research has been used in a wide variety of ways, such as encouraging plants to grow faster and better, and cows to give more milk. One experiment on plants showed that, exposed to rock music they wither and die, to classical music they thrive, and to baroque music they flourish and even wrap themselves around the source of the music!

John Diamond used music to help people heal themselves. He found that every musician works on particular problems within himself, using the music to express the way he works through the problems and finds a resolution. People then are drawn to the type of music which deals with the particular problems that they are concerned with, and the music helps them resolve these problems.

George Lozanov, a secret student of Peter Deunov in Bulgaria, discovered that certain kinds of music can greatly enhance learning, in particular Baroque music such as that of Vivaldi and Monteverdi; and he developed a highly successful method of teaching using music to accelerate the learning process. Originally this was called "Suggestopedia" and then "Superlearning" in English, and later "Accelerated Learning" in the USA.

Music, of course, appeals to the right-brain side of our nature, that side of our being which has been neglected so much here in the West, by the focus on left-brain training in our education. But the wonderful thing about this day and age is that we are discovering the importance of balancing these two, as Enrique Barrios demonstrates so clearly in his remarkably profound book, *AMI, Child of the Stars.*

Work is being done at the Monroe Institute and many other places on balancing the two hemispheres of the brain. PanEuRhythmy achieves this balance, so that we can then work, not as a split personality, but as a united, unified being, so that the currents of energy which rise through our being can connect at the highest point. As people are discovering from ancient Egyptian symbols, the energy that rises up the two sides of our bodies needs to make a leap to connect at the top, and, when it does, people experience illumination and that higher mystical understanding which enables them to make sense of life. I think this is something we are all working towards. The exciting thing is that, as we approach this critical stage in the development of the human race, the great challenge is for us to make that leap of consciousness which will lead us to a higher dimension. In this way any imminent danger turns into a blessing, because mankind can then become greater, more whole than ever before, and the Golden Age which has been prophesied can actually come about and we can experience the Kingdom of Heaven on earth.

As human beings, we live upright like trees, making the connection between heaven and earth. Trees and human beings are both upright, and as such are conductors of energy. PanEuRhythmy helps us conduct that energy in a free-flowing way.

Some beginners seem to think they can bypass the music and just do the movements, but I have to point out that they will quickly become bored, as one tends to with movements practiced mechanically for the sake of physical exercise alone, and they will totally miss out on the profoundly exhilarating, inspiring, renewing, and healing benefits of the PanEuRhythmy as a whole. In fact, it is my experience that it is those people who go into it with real depth of attention, studying every detail, and practicing it with totally absorbed consciousness, who continue to practice year after year, both alone and with others, and who derive such profound benefits from it that they come to regard it with very deep reverence and awe. (See Arleta Brzezinska's testimonial on page 36.)

Let me talk now more precisely about the PanEuRhythmy itself. The whole dance takes an hour and a half to perform. The first part takes three quarters of an hour, and is about the awakening of the human soul to its own potential.

Every single aspect of PanEuRhythmy is symbolic. Every movement is like a Japanese koan. It is something one can dance again and again, and each time penetrate more deeply into the understanding of its symbolism. I have derived my understanding of the symbolism of PanEuRhythmy from books by people who knew Peter Deunov, such as Yarmila Mentzlova and Viola Bowman, from working with Leon

Moscona (a Bulgarian mystic and spiritual teacher who worked with me for two years in England), and from my own evolving understanding of PanEuRhythmy through dancing and teaching it over the years. I have also traveled to Bulgaria and learned from people who have been dancing PanEuRhythmy all their lives, some of whom knew and worked closely with Peter Deunov for many years.

This is not a final statement of what PanEuRhythmy is all about, but simply a sharing of my own understanding, so as to kindle yours. If what I say does not appeal to you, just dance the movement anyway, as they are meaningful in themselves without explanation, and gradually you will evolve your own understanding of PanEuRhythmy.

PanEuRhythmy is usually danced in pairs, but is also profoundly beneficial danced alone. It is often easier to dance the earlier dances singly, especially in small groups or for the purpose of learning. Otherwise, throughout the PanEuRhythmy, we dance side-by-side in pairs, creating an inner and an outer circle, all moving counter-clockwise. The inner partner needs to remember to take smaller steps to ensure the outer partner is always able to keep pace easily..

The PanEuRhythmy is danced in a circle, counter-clockwise, with the music at the center, whether live musicians or a cassette player. Having the music in the center of the PanEuRhythmy circle is crucial. The music expresses and represents the source of all creation, since all creation has its origin in the sound emanating from the Creator. "In the beginning was the Word" could be translated as "In the beginning was Voice/Sound/God expressing." Our dancing in a circle expresses our relationship to the center, the Source, in a manner similar to the movement of the planets around the sun.

The counter-clockwise movement is also symbolic. The teaching is that, when the Divine spark incarnates on earth, the downward movement from Spirit into matter is clockwise. (We are talking symbolically, of course, because it is not really downwards, but we have to use symbols.) The cycle of movement from matter back into Spirit then is a counter-clockwise movement.

When we are thoroughly incarnate in our bodies in this universe, the day comes when we wake up and begin to question what life is all about. This is when we begin the cycle of evolution, of matter expanding into Spirit, with the cycle of evolution rising counter-clockwise. So

PanEuRhythmy, which is the dance of spiritual evolution, is danced counter-clockwise around the circumference of the circle.

Once we have danced the PanEuRhythmy in a circle around the center and formed our connection with the center of all Creation, we can then move on to dance **The Sunbeams**. Here we move in on radii towards the center of the circle and backwards out again, as if along the spokes of a wheel. We dance inwards and fill ourselves with Light and Love, and then dance outward from the center to bring this gift of Light and Love back out into the world. This is the dance of those illumined souls who know why they are on earth, who are no longer on this earth for their own benefit, but purely to transmit light and healing and goodness to other people. This is a path which I am sure we are all treading, to become Sunbeams radiating that love and goodness from the Divine source out into the world which is sadly in need of it.

The final dance is called **The Pentagram**. The Pentagram is a five-pointed figure, the symbol of Man, as in Leonardo da Vinci's drawing of a man standing in a circle forming a five-pointed star. The first five pairs in each "sunbeam" pivot to the right, standing now in lines radiating out from the center and facing counter-clockwise round the circle. As the music proceeds, all move forward eight steps. The two pairs who are the feet, move forward only eight steps and stop. The outer pairs, who are the hands, move on another eight steps and stop. The pair which forms the head continues on another eight steps (24 steps forward), and then stops. In this way we form a beautiful pentagram, a five-pointed star. As the music proceeds, we join up again, and then together sweep around, like an arm of creation. After that we form another pentagram, then join up again, repeating the sequence five times in all.

So you see the symbolism. We start on the periphery of life. When we wake up, we search to connect again with our Divine source and move on in the cycle of evolution, until we join those enlightened beings who can directly channel Love and Light from the Divine source out into creation. Finally, we take our place in the body of Cosmic Man, made in the image of God, and manifest the Kingdom of God on Earth, the fullness of the Divine in every realm of creation.

"Joyful Peace and Unconditional Love"

"When dancing PanEuRhythmy
and for a long time afterwards,
I feel a Joyful Peace and unconditional Love
inside of me and, surprisingly, also around me!
It is as if my physical environment is responding
to the vibrations of PanEuRhythmy.
I now feel that the more people practice PanEuRhythmy,
the more there will be peace in the world.
Once when talking with Ardella,
I told her I would like to participate
in spreading PanEuRhythmy in the world,
and asked how to be her disciple.
She just smiled at me and said that
I should allow PanEuRhythmy to be a part of my life
and: "Just keep dancing".
So, when dancing, I would meditate
on particular PanEuRhythmy gestures and think about
how PanEuRhythmy could become an integral part of my life.
I thought about what PanEuRhythmy meant to me,
and how I experienced it in the processes of my life.
While practicing, the answers started appearing .
At different moments in my everyday life,
appropriate Paneurhythmy gestures would come to mind.
For example, when I felt thankful for something,
"Clapping" came to mind.
When I felt anger, I visualized myself performing "Liberating".
When I feel ungrounded and blocked, I breathe more deeply
and visualize myself dancing "Jumping"
and being in touch with the ground.
The result is amazing!
Not only do I feel better grounded but also more joyful.
On the physical level, e.g. when I feel a sore throat,
I keep repeating "Evera"as a mantra, prolonging the vowel "e",
and this heals my throat-chakra.
In this way PanEuRhythmy has become integrated
into different aspects of my life.

Arleta (on the right)
with the Polish-Slovak mountains in the background

*I perceive PanEuRhythmy as a concrete tool
for dealing with different situations.
When I have some difficulties
or when I have to make an important decision,
I always find time to perform PanEuRhythmy.
This helps me distance myself from what is happening,
and, thanks to this, solutions and
answers come to me much more easily.
During my practice of PanEuRhythmy,
I started experiencing Love and Unity more often.
My life took on another dimension
and became much more joyful.
For me PanEuRhythmy is a wonderful and simple practice,
and exactly what I was looking for in my life.
I am very grateful to the Universe and to Beinsa Douno
for this Love-filled Sacred Circle Of Life."*

Arleta Brzezinska, Gdansk, Poland: January 2009

Section 1

The First Day of Spring

These first ten movements are called "The First Day of Spring." Spring symbolizes the awakening, both of Living Nature, and of the human Soul.

The symbolism goes further. The music is always in the center of the PanEuRhythmy circle, because music is creative. Peter Deunov always had an orchestra in the center of the circle. The music is in the center, because it is from the center of all creation that we are constantly empowered, that we are constantly created anew every moment.

In the early stages of the PanEuRhythmy the emphasis is on attuning our own individual vibrations with those of the Higher realms, so we do not dance too close to those around us. It is preferable to keep a space between ourselves and others corresponding to our outstretched arms.

Although we usually dance in pairs throughout the PanEuRhythmy, people often find it easier in "The First Day of Spring" to dance singly when learning or if there are only a few in the circle.

Before dancing, many people like to pray three times one of the formulas given by Peter Deunov, such as the High Ideal, expressed in this beautiful prayer of the disciple:

"May we have a heart pure as a crystal,
a mind bright as the sun,
a soul vast as the Universe and
a spirit powerful as God and
one with God."

We may also attune to Nature with this formula:

O kindly, luminous beings,
Guardians of this place,
Thank you for your hospitality,
And may God bless you!"

1. Awakening

Like a little fern in Springtime, each of us has an inner potential, a Divine spark within us, which is all coiled up, but unfolding. When the sun shines, the fern unfolds in the Divine light awakening its being and drawing out its inner potential. Each little seed has within it a power that is unfolding. An acorn which is buried under the ground, has within it all the strength and power, which, a hundred years later, will become a great oak tree.

As we unfold to that Divine light, we also take it in, just as when we eat and expose ourselves to food, we take it in and assimilate it. When we expose ourselves to new ideas and influences, we need time to allow those ideas and influences to penetrate our being and to mean something to us. So the first movement, the opening and taking in, is called **Awakening**, as it depicts the awakening of the human Soul.

The whole of life — everything in the universe — works in cycles. All the planets and stars move around the universe in cycles. We work in cycles of day and night, summer and winter, as well as birth, maturity, death and returning to Source to manifest again in some other way.

These first ten movements depict the initial awakening of each person to what life is all about. We gently walk in rhythm with the beat of the music, starting with the right foot forward on the 1st, 3rd, and 5th beats, and the left foot forward on the even beats. This is important. The arm movements are done to the regular rhythm of the body walking, rather as the delicate melodies of violin, flute and harp are performed against the backdrop of the bass rhythm of trombone, double-bass, bassoon, and percussion.

In this way, the human body mirrors the orchestra, and I have noticed that people's dancing of the PanEuRhythmy closely reflects their own ease of handling the different aspects of life — physical, emotional, mental, and spiritual. For instance, people who are very well grounded in their physical bodies will usually flow easily with the rhythm of the movements, particularly of the legs. Those who are highly sensitive to the spiritual dimensions will be delicately attuned to the subtleties of the arm and hand movements, and will engage their whole consciousness as they dance.

We start with the hands and fingers curled up on the shoulders, then, as we step forward with the right foot, our arms swing up and out sideways and our fingers uncurl and extend out horizontally. As the left leg swings forward, we again sweep the hands up and inwards, back to the shoulders, curling the fingers in again to the starting position. The arm movements are done in synchrony with the feet walking — the outward opening of the arms in a semicircle up and out to the horizontal sideways, as the right foot steps forward, and the return of the arms up and back down to the start on the shoulders as the left foot steps forward.

This outward motion of the arms to the movement of the right leg symbolizes the outward motion of the left brain connecting with the world around us, while the return of the arms, coinciding with the movement of the left leg, depicts the function of the right brain or feeling nature which draws us back to center and connects us with the whole.

As we move, we let the forward part of the foot drop gently and naturally as the knee is lifted. Then, as the knee is lowered, the foot will make contact with the ground from the front backwards, the heel being the last part of the foot to be placed on the ground before the weight of the body is transferred onto it. This minimizes shocks to the spine, nervous system and subtle bodies generally, and, as we know from the principles of reflexology, ensures stimulation to the higher parts of the human body before the lower.

Peter Deunov recommended this original way of walking as most beneficial, because it has a very uplifting effect on our whole body, mind, and feeling nature. The modern way of walking, heels first, actually jars the spine, nervous system and subtle bodies generally, as many people have experienced. I have been experimenting walking like this, toes first, and the effect is powerful. One feels as if one is a soul floating in this beautiful world, and that one is travelling in a vehicle, a beautiful body, but is not pulled down by it. This has a really liberating effect. One experiences being body, mind, and spirit all together, without being completely weighted down to the ground. The body then becomes alive, magnetized, and uplifted.

Pictures of fairies show them moving in this same way, elegantly lifting one knee at a time with toes pointing down. They are light beings, and in all these dances we can experience some of their bright, joyful qualities and lightness.

1.Description of Movements for Awakening:

(40 bars and steps)

A More Natural Way of Walking is practiced throughout the PanEuRhythmy. This is the original way of walking, (as practiced in all cultures where barefoot walking and running is the norm,) and Peter Deunov constantly recommended it as the most natural and beneficial. As the knee is lifted, the forward part of the foot drops gently and naturally. Then, as the knee is lowered, first the forward part of the foot makes a gentle contact with the ground, starting with the toes and the ball of the foot. The heel is then the last part of the foot to be placed on the ground, before the weight of the body is transferred onto it. This more natural and easy way of walking minimizes any shocks to the spine, nervous system and subtle bodies generally, and ensures that the reflexology points for the higher parts of the human body are stimulated first before the lower.

Starting position: We stand in a circle around the music, keeping a space between us corresponding to our outstretched arms. We turn to face counter-clockwise round the circle. Feet together, we turn our palms out and raise our arms sideways and up, fingers curling lightly into the palms, thumbs on the outside, until the backs of the fingers are lightly touching the shoulders close to the neck.

Bar 1: As the Right knee rises gently and the foot (toes first, then ball, then heel) is placed on the ground, the hands rise from the shoulders and spread out sideways, fingers pointing outwards in a horizontal direction.*

Bar 2: As the Left knee rises and the foot (toes first) gently touches the ground, the hands rise from the horizontal and retrace their path in a vertical semi-circle back to the shoulders, fingers gradually curling back into the palms on the way.

These steps are repeated for 40 bars. On the last step, in preparation for the next movement, the hands come together in front of the heart, finger-tips pointing up and lightly touching as in prayer.

---

* The palms may be facing up or down, with the symbolism changing accordingly. Peter Deunov first taught this movement with the palms facing up, then in later years was seen to have the palms facing down. Some groups choose to do it one way and some the other.

2. Harmonizing

Once we begin to awaken, we discover that we are literally out of harmony with ourselves. Before we can make further progress we need to harmonize our inner conflicts and dualities, so in the second movement we engage in **Harmonizing**. In the world of Spirit we are all one, because reality is one, but here in this physical world, we live in a world of dualities — black and white, male and female, thinking and feeling, day and night, conscious and unconscious, and so on.

We start this movement by bringing our hands together in front of the heart, because all harmonizing of unresolved problems takes place in the heart. Bringing our hands together symbolizes bringing together the thinking and feeling sides of our nature, the polarities of the right and left brain. Our fingers gently touch, and the healing energy flowing through our palms crosses the gap between them. When learning to give healing energy to others, we start by feeling the energy crossing the gap between the two palms. We bring the hands close to one another, so that the energy can flow between them.

Then, as our right foot steps forward, our arms swing out sideways to shoulder level. The movement is very free and easy. We just allow the arms to swing out sideways from the shoulders, out and together again. We find that the more we let ourselves go, the more our shoulders loosen up, our chest begins expanding, our breathing becomes freer and fuller, and our heart begins to open. We take in more oxygen, more prana (as they call it in the East), more negative ions, more healing energy, and so we begin to revitalize ourselves.

2. **Description of Movements** for **Harmonizing:** (30 bars and steps)

Bar 1: The Right foot springs forward (toes first,) and the hands sweep down from the prayer-position at the heart, and out sideways in a semi-circle till the arms are stretched out horizontally, palms facing down.

Bar 2: The Left foot moves forward, and the hands swing back down and up to the heart, finger-tips touching lightly and pointing upwards as in a prayer-position in front of the heart.

These movements repeat for 29 bars. On the 30th bar. in preparation for the next movement, the fingers turn toward the heart, (instead of touching one another.)

3. Giving

When we have established a degree of harmony within our being, we find our heart opening and we want to start **Giving**. Our heart flows outwards and we find ourselves wanting to share with others the riches of life that we have been discovering. Then, when we give, we find that the world wants to give back to us — other people, Nature, the Universe. So the natural flow of giving and receiving begins happening and eventually becomes an integral part of our lives.

The movement of **Giving** starts with the fingers lightly touching the spiritual heart center, located at the site of the thymus gland. To find the thymus gland, just follow the bony ridge which comes down from your throat into your chest. A little exercise you could do (separate from the PanEuRhythmy) is to tap lightly on the most pronounced bone of this ridge. You will find that this helps to wake you up and make you more alert. This is because it is the seat of the thymus gland, and also the spiritual heart center or High Heart. (The physical heart is lower and slightly more to the left.)

As the right foot moves forward with the first beat of the music, the hands lift forward and up from the thymus, while the arms and shoulders swing forward and stretch out horizontally with the palms up and pointing straight in front as if making a generous offering to someone. Then the left foot moves forward, and the hands sweep back up and round and back down again to touch the heart center. This rhythmic, swinging movement of the arms synchronizes with the steady pace of the feet throughout, and produces in the heart a deep feeling of giving.

3. Description of Movements for Giving:
(34 bars and steps)

Starting position: Left foot forward, palms and fingers gently on the heart, upper arms relaxed against the sides of the chest.

Bar 1: The Right foot steps forward, and both hands spring up and out from the heart, palms turning up, the entire arms and fingers reaching forward together toward the horizon.

Bar 2: The Left foot steps forward, and the hands, palms up, retrace their semi-circular path up and back to the heart, elbows dropping back to the sides of the chest.

These movements are repeated throughout the 34 bars.

4. Ascending/Climbing

The sculptures of Walter Russell, that great American genius, have the same exhilarating quality as in this movement of **Ascending.** After truly opening our being to **Giving,** the joy of life starts bubbling up within us in earnest. Life becomes too exciting and adventurous to stop at this point. We want to begin to ascend the heights, so we practice and develop discipline.

In this movement, **Ascending,** we reach our arms up at an angle of 22°-23° from the vertical, the same angle as the axis of the earth.. This angle, which is half-way between the vertical and the diagonal, is the same as that of a mountaineer climbing a steep ascent or a runner fully exerting himself. Yarmila Mentzlova quotes the Master Peter Deunov (among others) who talk of this as the dynamic and evolutionary angle of the body, since the maximum energizing and awakening takes place in the human body when it is leaning forward at an angle of 22°-23° from the vertical — the same angle as in Walter Russell's statues, as I noticed when teaching at Swannanoa Palace, his center in Virginia.

In **Ascending,** the upper and lower limbs of the same side of the body move together. This stretches each side of the body alternately, stimulating each side of the brain in turn, as in the sideways stretches of Hatha Yoga, except that, because they are done in a repetitive rhythm, we hardly notice the stretching.

Symbolically, this alternate stretching of the right and left sides of our body represents a reaching up first with our thinking nature, because our awakening generally starts when we discover some great idea. Our thinking nature is thus stimulated, and we reach up for more. Then our feeling nature, our heart, wants to follow. So our Ascending progresses with the thinking and feeling sides of our being alternately.

This dance is exhilarating, producing energy, vitality, and joy of body, mind, and soul.

4. Description of Movements for Ascending: (26 bars and steps)

Bar 1: As the right foot steps forward, the palms turn down and the hands move in opposite directions from each other. The right arm, palm facing forward, extends forward and up to a near vertical position, (22½° from the vertical according to Yarmila Mentzlova,) while the left arm stretches down and back in the same straight line as the right arm, palm facing back.

Bar 2: The arms swing past the sides of the body into the reversed positions, that is, left arm up and right arm down, and the left foot steps forward. In the last bar, while the left foot steps forward, the left arm stays down with the right arm, in preparation for the next movement, **Elevating.**

5. Elevating/Soaring

After **Ascending,** a magnetic momentum arises within us, and we find that the two sides of our being are working in harmony, leading us naturally into the next movement, **Elevating**.

It is interesting that a distinct emotional state called "elevation" is now being studied, in particular by a moral psychologist who writes that we come to this state of elevation through observing others — their strength of character, virtue, or "moral beauty." Haidt says that he first found a description of "elevation" while looking through the letters of Thomas Jefferson. Jefferson wrote of the physical sensation that comes from witnessing goodness in others: It is to "dilate [the] breast and elevate [the] sentiments and privately covenant to copy the fair example."

Haidt also quotes the first-century Greek philosopher Longinus on great oratory: "The effect of elevated language upon an audience is not persuasion but inspiration," evoking in us "a desire to make a difference, to become a better person, to lead a better life, opening hearts and minds to new possibilities." We are all very aware of how inspiring leaders, such as Martin Luther King, Nelson Mandela and Gandhi can uplift our whole consciousness and magnetize us into wanting to work for a better life for the whole world.

This dance, **Elevating**, also has this energizing effect and symbolizes the elevation of consciousness that takes place when people have been working on themselves for some time, and a powerful momentum is flowing in their lives. The two sides of their being, their thinking and feeling natures, are working together in harmony, and they are making accelerated progress in developing themselves as people and in elevating their spiritual awareness.

5. Description of Movements for Elevating:
(26 bars and steps)

When the music changes, both arms are down, palms facing back. Now both arms swing forward and up, as we move forward on the right foot. Then they swing back down again, as we move forward on the left foot. This swinging of the arms forward and up as the right foot steps forward, then down and back as the left foot steps forward, continues until the music changes again.

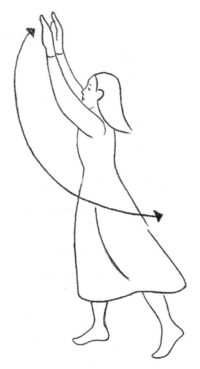

Bar 1: Both arms swing together past the sides of the body forward and up to the same near-vertical angle as in **Ascending,** palms facing forward and fingers extending up, and the right foot steps forward.

Bar 2: Both arms together swing down and back past the sides of the body, palms facing back and fingers extending downwards, and the left foot steps forward.

These movements repeat until the 26th bar, when the left hand is placed on the left hip, fingers forward and thumb back, and the right hand comes up in front of the chest, palm down, fingers together and pointing out horizontally towards the heart.

6. Opening

The next dance, **Opening**, allows us to expand even further, this time horizontally. This dance-movement denotes that we are opening up to the Universe all around us and outside the circle. Our right hand is on the outer side of the circle, which symbolizes that with our mind, the thinking side of our nature, we are opening up to the vast Cosmos around us. We are enlarging our minds, as if drawing back a curtain, and opening ourselves up to great ideas. As we move around the circle, with each sweep of the arm out, we are opening to a different part of the horizon, of the world, of the zodiac, of the great portals of Life.

This opening-out movement of the arms synchronizes with the forward movement of the right foot, symbolically expressing the function of our thinking nature moving out to connect with the world around us. The arm swings back to the heart, as the left foot moves forward, symbolically expressing the function of our feeling nature, which directs our attention inward to the heart and helps to develop our intuitive abilities.

To do this dance properly, the hand and arm need to be in a straight line, the elbow needs to be on a level with the shoulder, and the fingers must point to the spiritual heart center at the thymus gland. Some people call this the High Heart because the physical heart is a little lower down. This is the heart from the Spiritual point of view, and this is where we find the thymus gland, the heart of our being. The fingers point to the High Heart, without covering it, and you will notice that this causes us to open our chest wider. It gives us a powerfully expansive feeling, and as we swing the arm forward and out to the side horizontally we feel our consciousness going right out into outer space, into the Cosmos.

Halfway through the dance, when the melody rises higher, we change over hands. The right hand goes to the right hip, and now the left arm swings out horizontally, opening to the center of the circle — symbolically to the center and source of Creation. With the music we are rising higher. Our feeling nature is developing its intuitive capacities and attuning to guidance from the Source of all Creation.

As with Neale Donald Walsch, who wrote *Conversations with God* and *Friendship with God*, I have found that when doors close in my life, (and many doors have closed, some of them very painfully,) it is because I am being guided to something else which is greater and more important for me to do. If I just accept this, and work with it, the joy begins to flow again, and the meaning and purpose gradually become clearer within me.

In this second half of **Opening** we are opening up our heart to the Heart of Creation. Our left arm opens out to the center of the circle, where the music is coming from, and as we listen to that Divine Music, we hear the "distant drummer" setting the pace for our life. Then our left hand returns to the heart center, pointing to it without covering it. We are listening to our inner music, "the Song we came to sing."

Lawrence Le Shan cures people of cancer by helping them discover the "song" they came to sing, and John Diamond also talks of this. Each of us, deep in our inner being, knows that there is some great purpose for us in this wonderful world. When we can discover this "song," we can, as John Diamond said, "cantilate" and life becomes an incredible joy and an amazing song. When we open up with the feeling side of our nature to this music which is inspiring and guiding us, our life can then truly become a Song of Creation.

6. Description of Movements for Opening: (40 or 41 bars)*

On the last beat of **Elevating** the left hand is placed on the left hip, fingers forward and thumb back, and the right hand comes in front of the right chest, palm down and fingers pointing towards the heart, elbow out horizontally to the side.

On the first beat of **Opening** the right arm swings out horizontally from the heart forward and out to the right side, and the right foot steps forward. Then, as the left foot steps forward, the right hand returns in the same horizontal half-circle back to the heart.

* See "How PanEuRhythmy Evolved" and Appendix.

Bar 1: As the right foot steps forward, the right hand, palm down throughout, swings horizontally from the heart forward and out to the right side.

Bar 2: As the left foot steps forward, the right hand swings horizontally back to the heart, palm down, arm bending at the elbow and remaining horizontal.

These movements are repeated until halfway through the dance when the music rises higher. At this point (bar 19), the right hand moves to the right hip and the left arm swings from the heart out to the left, either as the right or as the left foot steps forward. (See appendix for further details.)

These last two movements continue to the end, when the two hands, as if gripping a rope or chain that is barring the way forward, meet in front of the solar plexus, ready to start the next movement, **Liberating**.

PanEuRhythmy as a cosmic, conscious dance

*I have experienced the beauty of PanEuRhythmy
as a cosmic, conscious dance.
To discover its depth and meaning takes time
and a realignment of oneself with the forces of Nature.
The physical energies come alive in the movement
and in so doing help us toward transcending them
and bridging the subtler cosmic energies.
When physical movement, feelings and thoughts are aligned,
one can experience a harmony that is ecstatic.
The process for me has included
dwelling on each of these three aspects separately
before experiencing a flow in which there was a unity.
These dances are truly a gift of Love
from our Master Peter Deunov,
a love for humanity which will enable us
to participate in our evolution
as enlightened citizens of the universe.*

Giselle Whitwell, USA and Bolivia

7. Liberating

When we have discovered our inner "Song," our true Purpose, we may find that there are things in our life stopping us from fulfilling this purpose, and we need liberating from them. So we have to return to our lower nature, to our power center in our solar plexus to release ourselves from all the negative patterns and emotions locked in there which keep us from fulfilling our life purpose. We have to break these bonds holding us back and liberate ourselves from negative programs, habits, and tensions, in order to fully and freely sing "the Song we came to sing."

Every movement in PanEuRhythmy acts on the subtler levels of our being and produces far-reaching effects. This particular one is very liberating and the movements have the effect of strengthening our willpower to really move forward with our lives. People often report that this is one of their favorite dances, as it frees up their power center.

In recent years I have found myself being profoundly inspired and strengthened by all the work that is being done in all areas of society, even in prisons, to liberate us all inwardly — through emotional release, understanding, forgiving, nonviolent communication, mediation and meditation. In the San Francisco Bay Area where I live I attend an annual celebration of the Worldwide Forgiveness Day Alliance where we hear from "Pioneers of Forgiveness" of how they have discovered profound inner liberation and joy, often after many years of deep post-traumatic distress, when they have been able to let go and truly forgive those who have hurt them. We meet people who have been severely injured physically and/or emotionally, beaten up, even tortured or imprisoned in concentration camps during the holocaust. It is so inspiring to hear their journeys to healing and how eventually they found it in their hearts to forgive.

One of these women, Jaimee Karroll, now works in our local maximum-security prison, San Quentin, with the Insight Prison Project where prisoners guilty of violent crimes learn to talk about and release their feelings, develop insight, then become more self-aware to the point of being able to control their impulses when triggered. This ability becomes crucial in enabling them to become fit for release back into society, and makes all the difference in their being able to avoid committing further crimes and hurting others again at any point in the future. Her own childhood experience of being severely attacked and beaten by three men enables her to open the way for such prisoners to work towards making reparation towards their victims and possibly being able to meet with others who have been victimized.

I know, too, another woman whose child had been murdered and who later was able to forgive the man and even visit him in prison. Needless to say, the effect of such incredibly loving forgiveness ripples out through both victim and perpetrator in ever-widening circles of healing in the world, liberating humanity for higher levels of life-experience and endeavor.

As we start this dance-movement, we take hold of imaginary chains in front of our solar plexus, our power center. We break them and throw them to the sides, flinging open our hands as we swing our arms out sideways to avoid throwing anything symbolically into the faces of those behind us. Throwing our arms to the sides also opens our chest and encourages full breathing (and avoids pushing our head and shoulders forward, as usually happens when we throw our arms back.)

Symbolically we are clearing the way forward, not only for ourselves but also for all those who will follow in our footsteps. When we free ourselves inwardly, we also free up those who follow after — our children and posterity generally. Then, liberated from our bonds, we can step forward into freedom.

7. **Description of Movements** for **Liberating:**
(40 or 41 bars)*

The hands form two fists in front of the solar plexus, fingers down and thumbs touching, (as described in Yarmila Mentzlova's book on PanEuRhythmy.) Depending on the choice made in **Opening,** the break and outward movement may occur on either the right foot or the left foot. However, it is also possible to make a one-step pause with the hands in front of the solar plexus to enable the break to be made as the right foot steps forward — as Peter Deunov may well have originally taught.

In one bar: The two clenched hands "break" the rope or chain at the solar plexus and fling the pieces out sideways as if clearing a path forward, the fingers opening out as if "flung" straight out to the two sides.

In the next bar: As the other foot steps forward, the two hands swing down and return together, fists clenching again in front of the solar plexus.

On the last step, the hands are out, ready to swing together in the next movement, **Clapping.**

*See **"How PanEuRhythmy Evolved"** and Appendix.

8. Clapping

The next dance is **Clapping,** which is how we often express our feelings of joyous thankfulness. The heart is now set free and we can fully be our true selves. The arms swing down from shoulder level and forward and, as our arms continue on up, we clap in front of the heart and our hands open upwards to form a chalice, symbolising how Gratitude can make way for Divine Grace to flow into our lives.

I am a linguist and like to look into the origins of words, as I find that they teach me a great deal about the true meaning of a word. The words "Grace" and "Gratitude" both come from the same Latin root. Gratitude is man's response to Divine Grace — which flows more easily into a heart filled with gratitude. This tells us that if we really want to progress quickly, the key is to be grateful — grateful for everything that happens, even when going through troubles, trauma and suffering. When somebody hurts us, we can respond by thanking that person or thanking the Universe for that suffering. We can "welcome every event

Clap!

as an advent," because every event can become an advent when we respond with gratitude. We clap with joy and look up, and our arms and hands open upwards, so that our hands, our hearts and our whole being express Gratitude and become like a human chalice opening to be filled with Divine Grace.

The upward gesture is only the first half of the movement. The downward gesture is equally interesting. Once we have received the Grace, we want to bring it down into every level of our being. A chalice has a long stem, but it is solid and nothing can flow down through it. We, on the other hand, are alive and can choose. We can keep the Grace we have received in our heads or we can choose to channel it down through our hearts and share it with all around us. As our hands and arms swing back down from the high point of the movement, they swing close to each other in front of the heart, palms facing each other without touching. In this way we form a channel through which the Grace can flow down through all levels of our being. The human Chalice can thus become a human Channel of Grace.

Our arms and hands continue on down and swing out sideways to form a horizontal line with the shoulders. This expresses the activity of the soul, opening itself to become a channel for Divine Grace to enter the earth and radiate out into the world. Gratitude opens us to receive Grace, and Grace opens the chalice of our being to become a channel of Divine blessing in the world.

The symbolism goes even further. This dance is number 8 in the PanEuRhythmy, and 8 symbolises fulfillment. 8 on its side is the infinity sign which represents perpetual motion. **Clapping** represents a point in our spiritual journey where we start experiencing fulfillment. This gives rise to deep inner rejoicing, for we feel we have begun to tap into the Fountain of Youth and the Source of perpetual energy.

8. Description of Movements for Clapping:
(40 or 41 bars)*

As the hands swing back together, they clap in front of the heart and then swing on up and open upwards in the shape of a chalice to receive a blessing.

In the next bar, as the other foot steps forward, the hands sweep down again, the palms this time passing close to one another without touching, (as if tracing a fine channel downwards,) and then continue their smooth flowing circular motion down in front of the body and out to the sides.

In alternate bars, and on alternate feet, the hands and arms swing together and up, and then down and apart.

As the music returns to the first melody (of **Awakening**,) the hands, after being stretched out sideways, swing back to a position just in front of the mouth, with the thumb and first two fingers touching and the other fingers extended out and up, in readiness for **Purifying**.

* See "**How PanEuRhythmy Evolved**" and **Appendix.**

9. Purifying

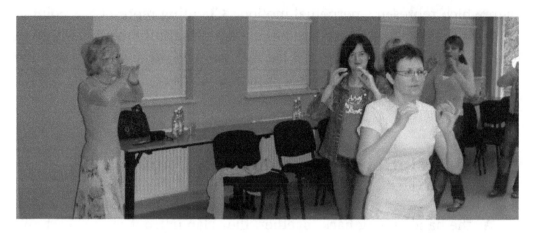

We begin this movement of **Purifying** by bringing together the first three fingers (representing the positive, negative and neutral energies) of both hands in front of our lips and, as we blow on them, our arms gently move out horizontally sideways, as if scattering seeds in the wind. The thumb represents Fire (associated with the Third Eye center), the index finger Air (the Throat chakra), and the middle finger Water (the Heart chakra), so we can see this movement as a purifying of the message of these three higher chakras, before giving it out into the world. Then in the return movement, through the sensitive spaces between our fingers, we receive the subtle energies of Nature into our own being which balance the energies we give out from our own center of higher creative expression at the throat.

Once we evolve to this stage of **Purifying** we are really learning to nourish others. From the experiences in our lives we have derived great wisdom, but this wisdom must be purified before it can be of real service. So Life gives us opportunities to work on ourselves to blow away the chaff and husks, so that others may benefit from the seeds of wisdom we are able to scatter. In this way we may inspire others, even when we are not aware of saying anything significant. The important thing is to work on purifying ourselves in both thought and speech, so that what we do and say is pure and can bear fruit, whether or not we are aware of it. As we purify ourselves we blow those seeds of wisdom out to others on our way along life's journey.

Through the first few dances, our energy has been progressively rising from the lower chakras and denser parts of our body, and now it is expressing itself through our throat center, as we make manifest the results of our inner working on ourselves. This Self-expression is the final stage in this first cycle of our spiritual journey. Our Soul takes charge and we can finally transcend attachment to mere physical existence and symbolically learn to fly.

9. Description of Movements for Purifying:
(40 bars and steps)

The hands return to the center, in front of the mouth, thumb and first two fingers joined as if holding seeds.

On the next step, we blow on the fingers as if scattering seeds in the wind, and the hands spread forward and out horizontally, fingers moving gradually apart, until the arms and fingers are fully extended out to the sides.

On the following step, the hands return gently back to the starting position in front of the mouth.

At the end the hands stay out in preparation for **Flying.**

10. Flying

The final dance of **The First Day of Spring** is **Flying**. When we have reached this stage we have, as it were, taken off. Having liberated ourselves from the grossness and resultant difficulties of our past, having awakened our finer nature and worked on ourselves consistently over a period of time (in all the ways symbolized by the first nine dances), we have now become sensitive to subtler realms of being. Our discerning ability becomes keener, and we can truly begin to operate in the supra-sensory world. In other words, we are no longer earth-bound and begin to fly beyond the confines of physical reality. We are in a body — yet not of the body. We are in the world and yet not of the world, as Christ said. We can now begin to move through life, no longer unconsciously at the mercy of everything, but consciously, as the pilot of our own vehicle for life and light and healing in the world.

The movements of **Flying** resemble those of a bird, and appropriately the main muscles to be used are those of the shoulders. This takes practice, but it is well to aim at a rippling, flowing motion travelling from the brain stem at the back of the neck, through the shoulders, the upper arms, gently through the elbows, and with subtle fluttering movements engaging the lower arms, wrists, fingers, and on out through the finger tips into the subtle emanations radiating out in the soft, ultra-visual colors seen by clairvoyants.

We have now transcended the physical; the soul is born, as it were, after its "ten lunar months" of gestation (symbolized by the ten movements of "The First Day of Spring"). We are now operating in the realm of the deva* the life-force or energy-level of all creation — which sustains the physical in living, manifest form and gives it consciousness and life. We are ready to engage now in **Everá**, the true Dance of the Soul.

---

* The Sanskrit word "Deva" means "Being of Light," and also encompasses the whole spectrum of Light-Beings of the Divine world. It is the word from which "Divine" and "Divinity" are derived. (cf. in Latin, *Deus, divina*; in French, *Dieu, divin*, etc.)

10. Description of Movements for Flying:
(30 bars and steps)

In rhythm with each footstep, the arms flutter gently out to the sides like wings flying, the energy flowing very fluidly out from the shoulders, through the upper and lower arms, out through the wrists, hands and fingers, and on and out into the environment in subtle flowing streams.

It is more graceful to raise (rather than lower) the upper arms on the first note of each bar.

When the music comes to an end, the arms slowly and gracefully float down and relax at the sides of the body.

PanEuRhythmy is a magical experience
*If magic has the power to transform
even the worst of situations into a blessing,
then Paneurhythmy is nothing short of magic.
With its graceful movements, beautiful music,
the tingling feeling in my bare toes
gently stepping on the grassy head of the earth
and in my fingers extending towards the sun,
this sacred dance has always given me immense joy,
put me in touch with my soul and with amazing friends,
has often healed my body of its aches
and cleared my mind of its worries.
It has always left me with the invigorating feeling
that I, my fellow dancers and the peaceful nature surrounding us
are so much more than meets the eye,
that with each step and each breath
we all vibrate in resonant rhythm with the Cosmos,
taking in its immense Love, Harmony and Wisdom,
and transmitting them all around us for the benefit of others.
What could be more magical than to be reunited
with your true Self, with your fellow companions,
with Nature and the Cosmos!*
Aneliya Dimitrova — *Chicago 2012
(Translator and editor of books by Peter Deunov)*

Section 2

Enlivening our Energy Centers

After the first ten movements of the **First Day of Spring,** there are eighteen more movements to the PanEuRhythmy, all danced in a circle counterclockwise around the center, where the music is. These eighteen movements can be divided into three groups, with the first six being an awakening and spiritualizing of the energy centers within our being. Clairvoyant people often see colors associated with these dances — a different color for each. Very often different clairvoyant people have seen the same colors for the same dances, which confirms to me that this is so.

When enough people are participating, it is customary to dance in pairs which creates an inner and an outer circle. The inner partner always needs to take smaller steps to ensure the outer partner is able to keep pace easily. In the movements where we face the center or face outwards from the center, partners will be one behind the other. When one does not have a partner, one may visualise oneself dancing with one's angel — quite an inspiring experience!

11. Everá

In **Everá** we learn to work with the energies of Love, Wisdom and Truth, the upper triad of the Pentagram.

Peter Deunov and all the great teachers of the world tell us that in the beginning there was one universal language. The story of the Tower of Babel in the book of Genesis describes how the first language became splintered off into many different languages, and the same kind of story can be found in the Vedic (wisdom) teachings of India and the Far East.

C. S. Lewis' science fiction books, ***Out of the Silent Planet*** and ***Voyage to Venus,*** tell of a man who was taken to visit Mars and Venus, and how he discovered that there was one universal language, but that until now the earth has been cut off and silent as far as the universe is concerned, (probably because whatever sounds we have produced have been more like a cacophony than a symphony.) PanEuRhythmy is teaching us to blend in with the symphony of life, to blend in with the one universal language.

The name **Everá** is from an ancient language close to the original universal language which Peter Deunov calls *Vattaan*. We do not know what it means, and, if we did, we could not express it in ordinary human language. For realities beyond the physical, we do not have adequate language. For example, people who experience leaving their body report that the reality they experience out of the body is such that you cannot express it in ordinary physical language, (which is created to express mainly material realities.) Our modern languages express physical reality fairly adequately, but are highly inadequate in expressing subtle and spiritual realities. So this word, **Everá**, is like a mantra: its sound expresses what it is. The sound expresses something which is beyond our left brain's ability to process.

It is interesting to note that this powerful mantra-like sound occurs in the name of the eleventh dance, since in numerology 11 is considered to be a master number. In **Everá** we have mastered the first cycle of evolution epitomized by the **First Day of Spring,** and are now moving on in our evolutionary journey to enjoy more complex, varied and subtle dances.

The dance speaks of how, once we have found our wings and learned to fly, we gain a great overview and there is an added dimension to our lives. We then have to learn to flow with the currents of life, just like a bird when it leaves the nest has to learn first of all to use its wings and then to flow with the currents in the upper air. If it does so, then of course it does not have to flap its wings all the time. Once it finds a current which is leading the way it wants to go, it can connect with the current. This may be a little difficult at first – you see it fluttering its wings – but then it just flows and glides on that current. When it wants to go somewhere else, it again has to flutter its wings, find a different current, and then flow with that current. This dance, **Everá**, is teaching us how to do this, how to launch ourselves from a purely physical life, to flow with the life of Spirit.

To begin this dance, we face the center of the circle, with our hands palms down reaching out to the left, connecting with the stream of Love. Love is something we experience through our heart, through our feeling nature. The circle is moving counterclockwise, so we are swinging forward as our hands swing to the right, our hearts opening to Universal Love which sustains and creates all that is. We then swing round and forward on our right foot, while our hands swing up toward our heart. Then, as we step onto our left foot, our hands reach forward and up. This gesture suggests a floating on and up on the wings of Love towards Truth.

As we swing our arms forward and up, we find ourselves turning outward from the circle towards our thinking faculty (symbolized by our right side) to connect with the stream of Wisdom. Love is the energy which creates all that is and gives us life. Wisdom gives us understanding of the great Laws of Life and Nature and radiates Light in the soul, illuminating the way forward.

We need the energies of both Love and Wisdom to steer us towards Truth, the ultimate goal of life. We flow with the current of Love on the left towards Truth, forward and up. Then we swing out and back to the right to link (through our thinking nature) with the stream of Wisdom. Carried forward, then, on this current of Wisdom from the right, we swing around to connect with our heart again, before floating, this time on the wings of Wisdom, forward and up towards Truth.

11. Description of Movements for Everá:

Starting Position: <u>Diagram 11a</u>: Standing facing the center, weight of the body on the Left foot, right toe extended to the right, arms extended to the left, palms down.

Bar 1: <u>Diagram 11b</u>: On the first beat of the music, the body swings forward onto the Right foot, turning into the counter-clockwise direction of the circle, arms bending and swinging up in front of the heart, palms either facing forward or facing each other a few inches apart.

Bar 2: <u>Diagram 11c</u>: Left foot steps forward and, palms still facing forward or each other, arms swing forward and up in a gesture of offering and receiving.

Bar 3: Body swings round and out, (so that one's back is to the center of the circle,) while the arms take a long swing down and back to the Right, palms turning to face the earth, and the weight of the body shifting onto the Right foot.

Bar 4: As in bar 1, but moving the weight onto the Left foot, as we turn forward again. (Movements are now reversed.)

Bar 5: As in bar 2, but stepping onto the Right foot.

Bar 6: As in bar 3, but turning back onto the Left foot to face the center again, as the arms swing back to the Left (as in the starting position.)

Everá
(as seen from inside the circle)

11a

11b

11c

The movements of these six bars are then repeated (the body turning alternately to face the center and to face out), ending with the arms extended forward and up at the end of the dance.

12. Jumping

The second dance, **Jumping,** expresses the joy we feel as we begin to appreciate the way Love and Wisdom are enhancing our lives. We stand facing the center, our hands and eyes raised up towards heaven, palms forward, in a gesture of awe and wonder. As the music starts, we bow down slowly to the ground in adoration, bending our knees slightly to avoid strain to the back. When our hands have nearly reached the ground, we swing our palms back to our sides and round to gather up the energies of Earth. Then, raising them up to heaven, we jump up and clap our hands above our heads.

I remember a man in one of my workshops who was very stiff and rigid like a plank of wood when he danced. When we danced **Jumping,** suddenly he was jumping like a three year old! We all jump like three-year-olds when we do this particular dance, but he just burst into giggles. He giggled and giggled, and the whole group started giggling with him. His whole body seemed to relax. Finally he told us that he was from Nicaragua and his father had been killed in the fighting there. His mother was so frightened that she used to keep him beside her and give him work to do all the time because she needed help with the younger children. From the age of three when his father died, he had never been able to play. He suffered from lower back pain, and one could see it; his whole body was rigid. He said afterwards, "From now on I'm going to dance PanEuRhythmy every day because it's loosened up my whole body. I feel I've regained my lost childhood!"

This dance is full of wonderful symbolism. Both men and trees have this function of connecting the material and the spiritual, and this dance depicts something like what happens when lightning flashes. There is a flash of electricity, of power, of energy, that goes from heaven to earth, from the spiritual to the physical. As we bow down in awe and wonder, we bring down that great Divine vision to the level of ordinary everyday life. Then, as we swing our hands back, we gather up the ordinary everyday things of life, swing our hands up, and, as we jump and clap our hands above our heads, there is that wonderful gathering up of the earthly, of the common everyday, and raising it to its Divine potential.

It is a wonderful dance for connecting Heaven and Earth.

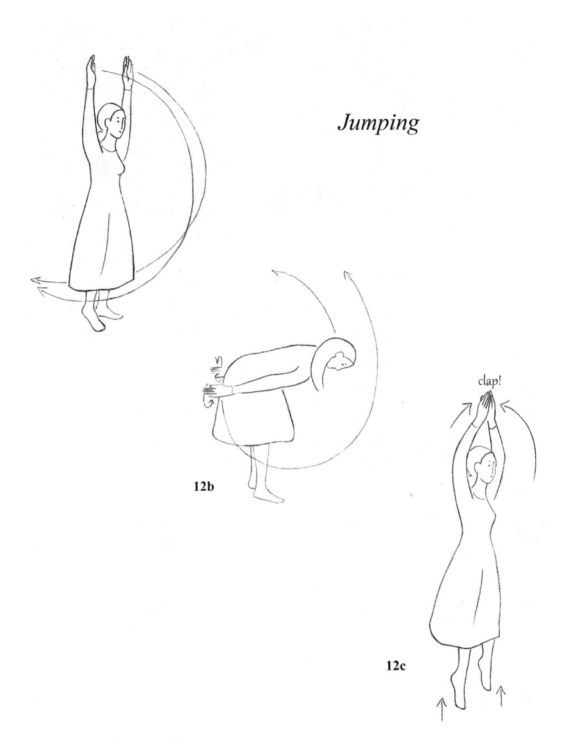

Jumping

12b

12c

clap!

12. **Description of Movements** for **Jumping:** (20 bars)

Before the music starts, all make a quarter turn to the left to face towards the center. (Paired partners will now be standing one behind the other.)

A. **Diagram 12a**: All raise their arms straight up above their heads, palms facing forward towards the center.

B. **Diagram 12b:** As the first five notes are sounding, the dancers slowly bend forward, lowering their arms forwards, down and then back. (To avoid undue strain on the back, it is good to also bend the knees slightly as the arms are lowered.) On the sixth and seventh notes the palms are rapidly turned forward and cupped.

C. Diagram 12c: The arms swing forward and up, while we simultaneously jump and clap directly above the head.

The palms then quickly turn to face forward again in preparation for the next movement down.

This movement is repeated five times.

13. Weaving

Now we move on to the dance of **Weaving** — weaving the tapestry of life. We take eight steps forward together, then eight steps sideways to cross over and change places with our partner.

Weaving is a gentle dance, very different from **Jumping**. Having established the vertical connection between Heaven and Earth within ourselves, we now move on to work on the horizontal connection, to weave harmony in our interpersonal relationships.

Weaving is the first dance in which we interact with others directly. As we move along on our inner journey, from working purely on ourselves to learning to interact with others, we go through a delicate process of becoming much more sensitive and adjusting to those who are around us. It is part of the process of learning to "love our neighbor as ourself," for only when we can truly love the self in the other, can we weave the fabric of life, and that is what this dance **Weaving** is about.

For the first time we interact directly with our partner in this dance and, if we don't have a partner, we visualize one. In a large group, the right-hand partner takes two steps forwards, so that, later in the dance, he can "weave" between his partner and the person immediately in front of him. In a small group, it is better to "weave" on the radius to and from the center, as we move sideways between the inner and outer circles. In this way we maintain our relationship with the center, which is crucial throughout the PanEuRhythmy.

We start by holding our elbows out horizontally, our hands palms down with our fingers pointing towards the heart center, again at the level of the thymus gland. Then, as we bring our right foot forward, our arms swing out, pivoting at the elbows until they are straight out sideways horizontally from the shoulders, palms down. We then swing them back to the heart as our left foot steps forward. In this manner, we take eight steps forward, parallel with our partners.

Remember that we are walking around the circle, each on our own radius, very close to the radius of our neighbors, yet on our own individual impulse of creation. Each of us is a Divine spark; each of us is incorporating, or manifesting, one ray of creation. So in this dance it is important to be very respectful of our partner. When dancing around the circle, those on the inside will have to take very small steps to enable those in the outer circle to keep up. This is also very symbolic of the way we have to adjust to our fellow travelers in our life's journey, and be sensitive and patient with one another.

This dance occurs in intervals of eight steps — seven steps forward, and then the feet come together on the eighth, (symbolizing completion, the eighth "step" completing the cycle and so moving us on and up to a new cycle in the spiral). This is meaningful because the number eight is the symbol of completion. There are eight colors in the spectrum (seven colors and then white, which is the blending together of all the seven colors of the rainbow), and eight notes in the musical scale (if you include the upper Doh, which completes the scale.) Even the form of the figure eight is meaningful and symbolic as it expresses perpetual motion.

A Spiritual Master, when giving his energy to a disciple (if the Master is a truly great soul and not acting out of selfishness) will send his energy out to the disciple in a figure of eight, around himself and then around his disciple, as expressed in Elizabeth Haich's book, *Initiation*. The master who is possessive and dominating with his disciple, will create a circle around himself and the disciple, so that there is bondage, as in a cult. A truly great Master will give complete freedom to the person who is learning from him, and so create a figure of eight.

Then we cross over: We take eight sideways steps, crossing over between the partners nearest us, on a direct radius between ourself individually and the center, and on the last step the feet come together. We move towards our partners with the foot which is furthest away. The persons on the inside circle will cross over to the outside, and those on the outer circle to the inner — like threads crossing over when weaving cloth on a loom.

In this dance we are weaving together the polarities of our life, harmonizing our inner marriage. Marriage is not an attempt to become one, in the sense of becoming uniform or identical. Marriage is the complementary interplay of two opposites — a harmony establishing itself between two very different people.

Similarly, the inner marriage is the marriage of the complementary opposites within ourselves: the conscious self and the unconscious, the shadow and the light, the male and the female, the thinking and the feeling, the right and the left brain. All these different aspects are not always easy to integrate within ourselves.

We have now taken the first steps towards going in toward our center, and learning to work with a partner. Working on ourselves with others also facilitates our connecting with the center of life, and accessing our Divine purpose and connection.

Weaving

13a

13b

outer partner crossing towards the center

13c

inner partner crossing away from the center

13. Description of Movements for Weaving: (60 bars)

All make a quarter turn to the Right to resume the usual counter-clockwise movement around the circle.

If there are a fair number of paired dancers, those on the outside take two steps forward, in order to be in a position to "weave" in front of their partners.

If dancing alone or with very few people, all may choose to do the sideways movements radiating simultaneously out from the center and back towards the center.

Starting Position: Arms raised horizontally, elbows out sideways, palms down, fingers pointing towards one another in front of the heart.

Bars 1-4: <u>Diagram 13a:</u> In each bar for four bars the following two movements alternate and repeat. In this way **seven forward steps** are taken and on the eighth step the feet come together.

In each bar, on the first beat of the music, the Right foot steps forward and the arms swing horizontally out to the sides.

On the second beat (third note) of the music, the Left foot steps forward and the arms swing forward horizontally back to their starting position.

Bars 5-8: The next series of eight steps (following without a pause) are taken **sideways, the partners "weaving" in and out of each other.** By the eighth step, when the feet come together again, the partners will have **changed places**.

<u>Diagram 13b:</u> In each bar, on the first beat, the **<u>outer partner</u> steps with the Right foot** in front of the left **towards the center**, then, on the second beat (the third note) steps with the Left foot sideways to the left, (also **towards the center.**)

<u>Diagram 13c:</u> Simultaneously, on the first beat, the **<u>inner partner</u> steps with the Left foot** in front of the right **away from the center**, then, on the second beat (the third note) steps with the Right foot out sideways again **away from the center.**

Bars 9-12: The movements of bars 1-4 are repeated but with the partners in opposite **positions**, and **moving forwards**.

Bars 13-16: The movements of bars 5-8 are repeated, the partners **moving in opposite directions, sideways** back to their starting positions relative to each other.

All these movements are repeated in each set of sixteen bars until the end of the music. At the end of **Weaving** the partners will have **exchanged places** relative to each other — the one who started on the inside will now be on the outside and vice-versa. Usually they will keep their new positions till the end of the PanEuRhythmy, but some groups prefer to return to their original places.

14. Think! / Missli!

Missli! pravo missli!
Missli! pravo missli!
sveshteni missli za jivota ti krepi!
sveshteni missli za jivota ti krepi!
krepi! krepi! krepi!
sveshteni missli za jivota ti krepi!

This next dance is one of those for which Peter Deunov himself created the words, so we like to sing these whenever possible. **Missli! pravo missli**! means: Think! Think right!

I feel this dance is showing us the true workings and full use of our faculties of mind. It demonstrates how true inspiration comes into our minds, and how it can then be made manifest in the world. When inventors and great geniuses make their discoveries, what seems to happen is that, just in a flash, a great idea comes to them. This does not usually just happen out of the blue, but after a great deal of work. A creative artist or scientist will often have to work and struggle and research for years and years before making a breakthrough.

Madame Curie was such a person. In order to do her research, she left Poland to study in France and worked extremely hard in very difficult circumstances. She was tested and challenged in every area of her life, until she finally made her breakthrough and proved the existence of radium and its power of radiation.

Mozart started very early in life. He would get a flash of inspiration for a whole symphony. Then he would meditate on that inspiration, before beginning to elaborate it and put it on paper. It would take him two weeks or more to be able to work out the whole symphony and write it all down. Finally it would take months to train the musicians to actually make that inspiration or symphony manifest.

A Divine thought can be transmitted in a flash to a person who is ready, but to actually make that thought manifest can take weeks, months, years, or sometimes a whole lifetime. That, of course, is our task as incarnate human beings in this world.

In **Missli!** we dance this symbolic moment of breakthrough by stretching both our hands up to the right, above our heads, with palms facing towards each other. We reach up, waiting for the music to begin, in order to connect with that inspiration from above. As we imagine and feel this inspiration being given to us, we receive it with gratitude and reverence symbolically in our hands, bringing them down on the right with very great care and attention. With our thinking faculty we bring that thought, that new inspiration down into the material, everyday, physical world. Then we take it into our feeling nature, our outstretched arms swinging across in front of the body and up to the left, and we connect with it at every level of our feeling and intuitive nature. We bring our hands down again on the left, and swing them back to the right and up again. Symbolically we are making sure our mind has fully comprehended all the levels of meaning. Then, and only then, can we begin to work on manifesting our new inspiration or insight and elaborating it in the outside world — the feminine aspect of the creative process.

In the next part of this movement it can be helpful to imagine a ball in front of our heart, a great beautiful supple ball of life. That ball might represent planet Earth, a particular dream or project, our own heart, or the circle of people we move among. The ball extends in front of us from the level of our throat down to the level of our navel. We pass our hands over it from the top around to the bottom, in a gentle caressing movement. We are putting out that new inspiration into the consciousness of mankind, into what Teilhard de Chardin calls the "Noosphere," the sphere of mind which surrounds our planet, Gaia.

With great love and gentleness and sensitivity, we encircle Gaia. We have to do it with gentleness and sensitivity, because new ideas often meet with great resistance, as we know from people like Galileo and others in the past who tried to communicate new ideas and met with resistance or persecution. Putting that idea out into the world now becomes our life's work.

At a certain point the music changes and our arms move out sideways and we gently stretch and press outwards three times with the palms of our hands. Sometimes this is called "upholding the pillars of thought." We reconnect with those pillars of thought which we have established between heaven and earth.

Another way of interpreting this gesture is that we are stretching out and enlarging our vision, which otherwise tends to narrow down as we become caught up in the complexities of everyday life. We take a moment to enlarge our vision, to keep our horizons expanded, to keep our sights universal and great.

Twice we interrupt the circling movement of our hands to make the three outward-pressing movements. Then we finish by resuming our circling movement (until the music stops and our feet come together), lovingly caressing our Mother Gaia.

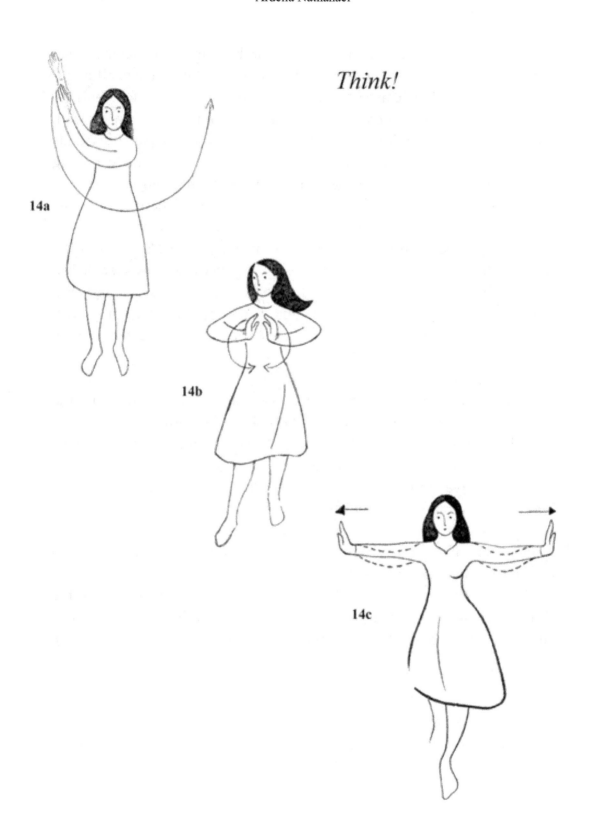

Think!

14a

14b

14c

14. Description of Movements for Think! (3 parts):

Part 1: <u>Diagram 14a:</u>
Standing still, feet together, throughout the first part of this dance, we start with the arms extended up to the right, palms facing each other or facing forward. (See "How PanEuRhythmy Evolved".)

With the first two musical notes for the word, **Missli!** (think!) the arms swing down, across to the left and up in a deep paraboloidal curve. Then, to the next four notes of the second phrase, **pravo missli!,** they immediately return in the reverse direction, finishing with a gentle little flourish or extension of the hands upwards.
This movement as a whole is done twice.

Part 2: <u>Diagram 14b:</u>
The music speeds up and changes. Starting with the Right foot, we walk forward to the music for the words: **sveshteni missli za jivota ti krepi**! At each step, the hands describe a circle in front of the heart and solar plexus.

Hands start over the heart, palms down, thumbs touching and fingers extended forward, and then move around and down to the solar plexus, as if caressing a sphere, until little fingers touch and the palms are up. The hands then relax and return up through the middle of the sphere to the top to repeat the circling movement briskly with each step.

Part 3: <u>Diagram 14c:</u>
The word, **krepi**! (keep! maintain!) is sung three times on a low note, while the arms extend out sideways in three gentle outward-pushing movements, (palms facing out and fingers pointing vertically upward.) The hands then return to the above circling movement in front of the heart and solar plexus.

This whole three-part sequence is then repeated.

15. Aoum

"Aoum, Aoum, Aoum, Om, Om, Aou-men"

Aoum is a very powerful and sacred sound. It tells the story of the origin of sound and its creative power. We can hear sound long before birth as well as after death. Sound is also the creative energy through which Creation happens. All the great traditions of the world teach that Creation happens through sound. *"In the beginning was the Word..."* is a clumsily translated Greek expression which could also be translated, *"In the beginning, God or the Divine Principle expressed itself."* *"In the beginning there was a vibration or sound."* In the Sanskrit scriptures of India, there is a similar phrase, "In the beginning was Vac (*Vaatch*)" which means *"voice"* or *"sound"* or *" word." "In the beginning was the Word."*

We know, just from a scientific point of view, that Creation happens through sound. If you strike a tuning fork and put it on a sand tray or in water, immediately its sound will form a pattern. Each sound has its own unique pattern. In C. S. Lewis's **Narnia** stories for children, the story of creation through sound is described in allegorical form. We hear how Aslan sang, and how with each different note he sang, different flowers, different trees, and then animals came into being. This profound truth is known to us both through allegorical and scientific means. Creation happens through vibration, through sound, through music.

Stephen Halpern and scientists have researched and discovered that our planet vibrates at just under eight hertz, (eight cycles per second.) Experiments have been done with plants, putting them in rooms with different types of music. The music under whose vibrations the plants flourished best was harmonious music. Discordant music caused the plants after a while to wilt, grow sickly, and even die. So music has a very strong influence. Plants flourish under the right kind of music, and animals as well. As we know, cows will produce more milk and plants will grow faster with harmonious music.

Scientists, recording different people in various activities and states of mind, found that one person whose vibrations corresponded very closely to the vibration of the planet was a powerful healer in the act of healing. This shows that a healer, by putting himself or herself in tune with the planet, acts as a kind of musical instrument through which the music of the Universe can be played and then transmitted to the person needing healing. It reminds me of the idea that we are the flute created to play the music of Love, (as in the story of Krishna in India.)

Aoum is one of the most sacred and majestic dances in the PanEuRhythmy. It is a beautiful sound which is found in many ancient traditions. In the Christian tradition we have it in the sound *"Ah-men."* In Egypt it takes the form of *"Ah-mun"* or *"Ah-min."* We find it in India in the holy mantra *"Om"* which is called the mother of all mantras. Only the hermits in caves in the mountains would use this mantra, because it is so holy it can lead us back into the unmanifest.

It is very interesting to look into this sound. It is in three parts: *Ah, Oo, and Mm* — in fact, it actually breaks into four parts, because after the *Mm* there is silence. If one looks at this closely, it's fascinating.

Ah is the first sound we make when we open our mouths and allow our vocal chords to express themselves. So *Ah* is that first of all sounds. It is the first sound, Alpha, in the Greek alphabet; in fact, all the alphabets I know start with the sound *Ah*. If you say easily and naturally "*Ahh*," it seems to express awe and wonder, a sense of "Ah! Wow! What a magical, wonderful universe we're in!" It is the excitement of waking up. It is also the energy of Spring. In the Hindu tradition, the trinity is made up of Brahma, Vishnu, and Shiva. "*Brah-ma*" is the expression of that first sound, *Ah*, the energy of Spring, of the expansion of creativity in the manifest world.

The second sound is *Oo*. It is formed through restricting the sound *Ah* by bringing our lips together. This is the sound of Vish-*nu*. Vishnu may be compared to Christ, for he is the manifestation of Love, or the Nurturing Principle. It is the ripening of fruit. Whereas in springtime the plants open up, spreading their leaves and their energy in all directions, in summer they concentrate their energy on the inner work, producing flowers, fruits, and ripening to maturity. If you listen attentively to that sound, *Oo*, there is that sense of fruit ripening in it, juice, oozing—that sense of "*Oo*," indulging, enjoying, revelling in the fruit, in the beauty of the creativity of Nature.

Mm is the third sound, the sound of satisfaction. It is also the sound we produce when we close our lips at the end of the sound. *Ah* is the opening; *Mm* is the closing. We have that in the *Omega* of the Greek alphabet, the *Alpha* and the *Omega*, the first and the last sounds. So *Mm* expresses the satisfaction of harvest, of a job well done, the end of the day, and the end of the year, the Thanksgiving holiday in the United States. *Mm* is the sound of satisfaction when we have finished eating and are enjoying what we have received. The final sound *Mm* is the sound of Shiva, who, in the Hindu trinity, dissolves the manifest creation back into the unmanifest.

After the three sounds comes the silence of the unmanifest — under the blanket of snow of Winter. After the satisfaction of the day, of the evening meal, we move into the silence of sleep, and in that silence our energies return into the unmanifest to renew themselves and be made ready for the next cycle of living.

When a tree or any other life-form has performed its function, as when a fruit is ripe and has shed its seed, it starts decaying in the soil. This is the natural cycle of dissolving, or returning into the unmanifest, that which has served its purpose. So the last sound is personified as Shiva, the dissolver — not the destroyer, as we say in the West, but that

which takes back into the unmanifest all that has served its purpose, so that it may prepare for even greater usefulness in the next Springtime of Creation.

We have to understand this dissolving. We saw a lot of dissolving in the twentieth century, the dissolving of Apartheid and the Iron Curtain, the dissolving of many forms and ideas which had served their purpose and were no longer useful in the world. Women now are particularly experiencing this with the old ideas of marriage. There is a new pattern of marriage: the woman inspiring a new vision and the man so inspired with this vision that he lends his strength to enable the vision to come into manifestation. More and more women are becoming the inspiration to their menfolk, and the men, full of admiration, are ready to lend their energy and their strength to support a woman who can really inspire them.

Shiva is the mystic in us, the returning from physical manifestation back into spiritual unity with God. The word "mystic," starts with mm, and that dissolving sound is the sound *Mm*.

These are the three basic sounds: *Ahh*, *Oo* and *Mm*. When these sounds are said together, *Ah-Oo-Mmm*, as *Aoum*, this is the sound which embodies all sound. **Aoum** is a mantra, a sound from the universal language, which will put us in tune with the Divine. Many people use it as a prelude for meditation.

Furthemore, the whole Sanskrit alphabet is based on these three sounds. From the opening of the mouth, the uttering of the first *Ah*, in the throat, the guttural consonants are formed: *k* and *g*. As we modify the sound into *Oo*, other consonants are created. Then the final closing sound, *Mm*, gives rise to consonants like *p* and *b*, which we call the labial sounds, because, like *Mm*, they are formed with our lips.

In this movement of **Aoum** our arms swing alternately up forward, and then back down, at 45º angles (different from the steeper angle of **Ascending.**) This diagonal position enables a balance between the physical and the spiritual worlds, between the energies of Heaven and of Earth. As we balance on the ball of one foot, while the other is extended straight out behind in the same diagonal line, the whole body seems to be aspiring upward and momentarily floating in the air.

The essence of this movement is Balance. We enter into balance with ourselves and our own Soul. This movement challenges us to enter into an exquisite balance physically, emotionally and Spiritually, in order to attune to the Divine.

We also chant as we move, which makes it even more powerful and beautiful. We chant *aoum* three times, then twice *ohm, ohm,* and finally *ah-men*, as in the West. This is the beauty of this dance — it blends together the East and the West; it blends together all the great wisdom-teachings of the world in one great symphony of sound.

15. Description of Movements for Aoum:

As we move we chant, *"Ah-oom, ah-oom, ah-oom, ohm, ohm, ah-oo-men."* (Two spellings are given to help the reader attune to the actual sounds.)

Chanting "*ah-*" on the first short note and keeping the body vertical (not leaning forward), we step forward on the Right foot, and extend the Left foot back until only the toes are touching the ground. At the same time the straight Right arm rises slowly in a semi-circle forward and up, and the Left arm extends the straight line to the back, palm facing back.

Chanting "*-oom*" on the first long note, the Right arm continues on up till it reaches a 45˚ angle, the palm unfurling up in a gentle wave motion to face forward and the fingers stretching out to continue the upward extension, while the Left arm and fingers continue the 45˚ line down at the back, palm facing back.

15. Aoum

"Aoum, Aoum, Aoum,
Om, Om, Aou-men"

Simultaneously we rise up, if possible, on the ball of the Right foot and, engaging the lower back muscles to enable us to maintain our balance, we extend the Left leg, foot and toes back and off the ground in one straight line. There is a delicate moment of pause in this position of exquisite balance, before we slowly descend again onto our Right heel.

Chanting "*ah-*" the second time, the Left foot now slowly steps forward, and the arms swing slowly past the body to exchange places, as we repeat the movement inversely.

These movements repeat seven times — with legs and arms alternating — the last two times to the two syllables of the word, "*aou-men.*"

Chanting throughout, **the whole sequence of seven movements is repeated four times as the melody is played four times**, making a total of **twenty-eight movements in all**. At the end, the feet come back together and the arms slowly and reverently return to our sides.

16. The Sun is Rising

"Izgrehva Sluntsehto
Prashta Svetlina
Nossi Radost zah zhivota tyah.
Sila zhiva izvorna techoushta.
Zoun mehzoun
bihnom tohmeh toh."

The words of this dance, **The Sun is Rising,** were also given by Peter Deunov himself. The first words "izgrehva sluntsehto" mean "the sun is rising." This lovely word "Izgref," meaning "Sunrise," was the name given to the community Peter Deunov founded in Sofia. (The word, Sofia, or Sophia as it is written in the West, means "Wisdom," and I feel that, too, is no accident!)

The garden which was at the center of Peter Deunov's community still exists and is well worth visiting. It is an oasis of peace and tranquility, deeply conducive to meditation.

Peter Deunov's body was buried in the center of this garden in an oval flower bed. It is marked only by the sign of the Pentagram, with its five lines representing Love, Wisdom, Truth, Justice, and Goodness, the five esoteric steps in the Divine school of life.

The last words of this dance, **The Sun is Rising,** are not in Bulgarian, but in the ancient language *Vattaan.* They are, "Zoon meh-zoon, zoon meh-zoon, bih-nom toh-meh toh." We don't know what they mean, but Peter Deunov has said that, when we are feeling low, it helps to use them as a little song or mantra, as they have a revitalizing quality.

Once the fountains of living water have risen up in our being, and the streams of energy rising up the two sides of our bodies have met in arcs at the crown, the heart overflows. Then we sing "Zoon meh-zoon, zoon meh-zoon, bih-nom toh-meh toh."

In contrast to Aoum (ah-oo-mm) which takes us to a transcendental state, almost a mystical connection, this mantra has an enlivening quality. These words open the heart and bring the bubbling fountains of living water up within us.

In order to evolve we must work first of all on our lower energy centers, our lower chakras. Once we have laid the proper foundation, we can then work on the higher energy centers starting with the heart. When the heart is truly open and working in harmony, the inner Sun of our soul can rise.

We are told that the physical sun that we can see is just a material counterpart of a much greater reality. The energy which has created the world is like a Cosmic Spiritual Sun — quite beyond anything we can see or visualize or even imagine. It has a subtle counterpart, and the physical sun we see is an even lesser counterpart. So there are, as it were, three levels of sun.

As we dance, we can visualize the physical sun at the center of our universe rising. Or we can take it to a deeper level and visualize the Cosmic Spiritual Sun rising within our being, rising in the consciousness of all creation, rising and taking its rightful place in the center of all things, becoming the Conductor of the great Symphony of Life.

The Sun is Rising

16a

16b

16c

16d

16e

As in **Weaving,** we start this dance with our fingers pointing towards each other at the heart center and with our elbows out sideways. We take a slow step with the right foot, visualizing the sun there before us in all its glory, rising gently over the hilltops. As it rises up in the sky, our arms rise up slowly until they are directly over our head, our fingers pointing up and towards each other forming the apex of a triangle.

Next we turn our palms out, and, as we bring the left foot slowly forward, we move our arms outward to a horizontal level — the sun sending its rays out into the furthest parts of the universe. Light overcomes darkness, and everything is raised to Divine perfection.

After this we turn our palms forward, and, stepping forward with our right foot, our arms sweep expansively forward and around and back to the heart. We slowly gather up all that wonder, all that joy, all that new life, vitality, inspiration and bring it gratefully, reverently, tenderly into our hearts. The whole sequence is repeated once more, starting on the left foot.

Once our higher energy centers are truly functioning, our lower chakras are brought into play more fully, and we become more fully realized beings. Our hands drop down by the sides of our bodies and make six little upward-springing movements, palms facing forward and up. These symbolize the fountains of living water, joyfully bubbling up within us. This is a wonderfully uplifting and revitalizing dance. Four times we do these six upward-bouncing movements, raising the energy all the way up to our heart, as fountains of living water gushing up and revitalizing our whole being.

Finally our hearts overflow in the final movement of this dance (which is very similar to Movement 3: **Giving.**) Our hands move in a semi-circle up and out forwards from the heart, palms up, and, as we take each step, we give and receive, we give out and we take in. We then pause for a moment, before repeating the whole sequence from the beginning.

The words for "The Sun is Rising" were given by Peter Deunov himself, so it is good to sing them in the original whenever possible, but one can also sing in English, as follows:

"The sun is rising now,
sending brilliant light,
filling life with joy and pure delight.
Living power, springing, flowing power,
Living power, springing, flowing power.
Zoon meh-zoon, zoon meh-zoon, bih-nom toh-meh toh.
Zoon meh-zoon, zoon meh-zoon, bih-nom toh-meh toh."

16. Description of Movements for The Sun is Rising:
(70 bars) (Three parts following on from one another without break.)

Part 1:   **Starting position**:   Finger-tips in front of heart, palms towards the body.

Bars 1-4: <u>**Diagram 16a:**</u> Singing "Izgrehvah sluntsehtoh," the Right foot slowly steps forward, toes first, and we rise up on the balls of our feet, as the hands rise slowly in front of the face until they reach a comfortable position above the head, middle fingers touching and forming an arc over the head, and the Right foot then comes to rest.

Bars 5-7: <u>**Diagram 16b:**</u> Singing "Prashtah Svetlinah," the Left foot gracefully and slowly steps forward, toes first, as the hands turn to face out and up and start moving out sideways. We rise slowly onto the balls of the feet, as the arms slowly spread out and down to the horizontal, palms down. The feet then slowly descend to the ground.

Bars 8-12: <u>**Diagram 16c:**</u>   Singing "Nossi radost zah zhivota tyah," we slowly step forward on the Right foot and then rise onto the balls of the feet, as the palms turn to face forward and the arms slowly and spaciously sweep forward, as if to include all of Creation within their scope, ending in front of and pointing to the heart.

The movements of Part 1 are then repeated with opposite feet leading, i.e. Left, Right, Left.

Part 2: <u>**Diagram 16d:**</u> **Sila zhiva, iz-vor-na teh-choush-tah**
The pace of the music quickens and the steps become more rapid and dancing in quality. The hands drop to the sides and the fingers bend forwards. The arms and elbows remain close to the body while, at each double note of music, the hands bounce progressively upwards in small bobbing movements, like water gushing up in a fountain.

Part 3: <u>**Diagram 16e:**</u> **Zoun meh-zoun, bi-nom toh-meh toh**
In rhythm with the music and our footsteps, we sing "Zoun meh-zoun, zoon meh-zoun, bih-nom toh-meh toh," alternately stretching our hands and arms (in an upward semi-circular movement) up and out forwards, then returning them (in the same semi-circular path), elbows dropping back close to the body and fingers to the heart.

(See **How PanEuRhythmy Evolved** and appendix re variations in part 3.)

"Refreshing of my mind and soul."

"I met Ardella Nathanael at a Congress in Sao Paulo in 1995.
From the first time I saw her - a radiant and energetic woman
— I was deeply touched. Since that moment,
I have been practicing PanEuRitmia to be in touch with the
Universe, to renew my strength and to refresh my mind and soul.
In 1996, I had the pleasure of hosting her
and I saw a true miracle.
I was teaching in a public school where the students' behavior
was normal but not the best among children.
There were many social issues that caused them to be
aggressive, defiant, loud and rebellious, etc...
Ardella came to my school one day
and gave a session of PanEuRitmia.
It was a great surprise for me and for the other teachers,
even the principal was amazed to see the students
dancing the wonderful "Dance of the Soul" — in silence
and performing all the movements with joy and pleasure.
t was an extraordinary experience and since this day,
when I feel the need to change the behavior of the students,
I dance PanEuRitmia with them!
Thank you, Ardella, for all the knowledge you have given me."
Ana María da Costa, Brasil

"Sacred geometry revealed in movement,

in sound, in dance, in the sunrise, "Izgreva Sluntseto"...
I had spent so many years longing
for this marvelous dance of the PanEuRhythmy...
The best moments of my life had been those spent dancing it
at Le Bonfin in France and at Videlinata in Switzerland —
until I had the good fortune to meet Ardella on a trip to Bogota
and be invited to her wonderful seminar
on this Dance of the Soul.
Listening to her story, I could see this sensitive and extraordinary
being of British origin in Bulgaria
learning this dance of PanEuRhythmy - in my opinion
one of the most valuable bastions of spirituality of this epoch.

It was in her seminar that I was able to experience
and better understand the movements,
and the hidden depths of inner meaning
within this legacy of the Master Beinsa Douno.
All my gratitude to Ardella for being an ambassador for
PanEuRhythmy and bearer of these teachings of joy, wellbeing,
spirituality and harmony in these tumultuous times.
Thank you for reminding me and bringing me once again the
power of "Izgreva Sluntseto," the Rising Sun
of the Dance of the Soul,
of the Sun born in the heart,
of the sun of the geometry and precision of life within Life
and especially in PanEuRhythmy,
in the rhythm of Being and spiritual elevation,
and in the understanding of one's personal rhythm
in alternation and consonance with the rhythm of the Universe.
With all my gratitude for the beauty, refinement and love
which you put into your teachings, dear Ardella.
It was a great honor to be your student.
I am still moved by your teachings and the memory of each step
in this extraordinary dance of the soul."

Jose-Miguel Riviere, Bogota, Colombia, 2010

Section 3

Spiritualizing the Elements

The ancient Greek tradition of Socrates and Plato talked of the universe as being composed of five "Elements," Earth, Water, Air, Fire and Ether/Akasha, which correspond to the five levels of vibration of matter in the universe: solid, liquid, gaseous, fiery and spiritual. I find it interesting to look at the next five dances in the context of these "elements" as a way of understanding them more deeply.

When we connect this third set of movements with the five elements: Earth, Air, Water, Fire, and Ether/Akasha, we find that they are showing us how to tune in to the spiritual essences of each, and so raise the consciousness and potency of each to manifest more powerfully at a subtler level of being.

17. Square

In this third section of the PanEuRhythmy where we are working to spiritualize all the levels of Nature, we could see this first movement, **Square**, as representing the spiritualizing of the "element" of Earth. **Square** is a very foursquare, earth-based dance, so we could say it is dealing with the densest of the elements in the ancient Greek tradition of Socrates and Plato: Earth or solid matter.

Each pair of dancers outlines their own "square," by moving first on a radius towards the center, then on a short concave arc round the center, then on a radius away from the center, and finally back round on the outer, convex circumference of the circle... It immediately becomes evident that the "squares" are not truly square, for each has two straight sides which are not parallel as well as two curved sides! They would resemble slices of a Brandt cake or sections of a tyre (arranged evenly around the hub.) Matter is said to be represented by a cube and Spirit by a sphere, so one could say that this square being drawn into a circle represents matter in the process of being spiritualized.

As in **Weaving**, we start with our hands pointing towards our heart center, elbows out to the sides, and again work in close collaboration with our partners, for in materiality we can only work effectively by transforming our relations with others. Again the partners are totally equal. We relate to each other from many different directions, and end up changing places in the dance. The important thing throughout is that we work synchronistically together.

Let us look further at the symbolism. The way I see it is this: when we incarnate, we are catapulted out into the outer circle of Creation where we find ourselves foursquare in matter, in physicality. But as children we are still "trailing clouds of glory... from God, who is our home" (as William Wordsworth wrote in his famous *Ode on Intimations of Immortality.)* We still have the consciousness of where we came from. We retain that intuitive awareness.

The ancient Vedic (Wisdom) tradition of India describes human life as having four stages: childhood, apprenticeship, adulthood and Vána-prastha (the forest stage, when we give up all worldly commitments and possessions and move into the forests as hermits to prepare for transiting out of this life and into the next). These four stages seem to correspond with what we are experiencing as we move round the four "sides" of our "square."

At the beginning of **Square** we are facing the center just as, in the early years of our life, we are facing the Light. We are joyfully going towards the center of the circle, the Source of all life. When we are not fully aware of the Source, we have our parents to represent it for us, so all is well and we can joyfully make our way towards the center.

We then turn left and start moving in an inner circle, corresponding to the stage when we need teachers (other than our parents). In the ancient tradition of India, children are, until puberty, in the care of the teacher, the "guru." Gu=darkness and Ru=light, so a guru is one who can lead you from darkness into light. Here we move in a clockwise direction (the cycle of In-volution), which symbolizes our becoming more and more involved in matter, in this world, in the ordinary things of everyday life. A true spiritual Teacher can initiate us into the Inner

Circle, where, close to the Center, the Source of all life, we can learn how to apply this knowledge to our human experience.

Then there comes a point when our education is finished and we have to turn our backs on the source and go right out into the world. This is like the teenager-to-adult stage, when we have to leave all that has been helping us until now — our parents, our background, even perhaps our spiritual tradition. I believe this is why young people sometimes rebel against their parents, turn to drugs, and try everything — because they have to make this journey on their own, away from the Light at the center, away from the Divine music, the center Source, the home, out into the outer darkness. If, in their preparation with their parents and Teacher, they have successfully internalized the Light, they can now move out into the darkness confidently, spreading the Light wherever they go.

The final stage is again counterclockwise (the cycle of E-volution), around the outer circumference of the circle. We evolve out of this life by completing all that we came here to do, and by attuning to eternity and Spirit in preparation for moving on to the next stage of Life. In our later years we find ourselves wanting to complete whatever we were not able to complete earlier on in our life's journey. This is important so that we can move on freely to the next stage of our Soul's evolution awaiting us after passing on from this life.

We can also look at this from another perspective. It is said that we go through all the signs of the zodiac, and usually it is not until we have gone through all of them that we wake up and begin to ask ourselves, "What is the purpose of life; what am I doing here?" We then have to go round them again, this time in the other direction — counterclockwise. This second time around, if we are awake and conscious, then we are truly on a path towards becoming Masters. We have the opportunity to move on towards the higher echelons of the human race. We are no longer just victims or ordinary human beings, living in a partial way, (not fully manifesting all that we are capable of being and came here to do,) but instead are fully in charge of our own lives and in tune with the greater World Vision, (as described in *The Celestine Prophecy* and *The Tenth Insight*.)

In **Square**, we go around twice. We come back to where we started, and then again we move towards the center. Perhaps our cockiness has now been knocked out of us, but in any case, if we are going to complete this task of incarnation satisfactorily, we are going to have to wake up and take note.

I see this as a picture of what happens in life. We have to go twice round the zodiac, so we go twice round the square. If we have awakened after the first time round, we can really achieve mastery of life and Self-realization the second time around.

When we move around the second time on the inner circle, even though we are going on the path of involution, we are hopefully doing it with greater consciousness. We more fully take in all the Light, Direction, Love and Wisdom that come from the center, so that, when we have to turn our backs on the Light, we can this time really confidently take the Light out into the world. We can face the darkness because we have internalized that Light, that Vision from the center. Then we can complete the circle, complete our work and be ready to move on to more subtle levels of being and work.

Incarnation into solid physical matter brings great challenges, and most of us need to go through all this more than once to get it right. Once we do get it right, we can raise the consciousness of earth, and the earth can become a paradise. Our human bodies can become subtle bodies, just as Elijah managed to transfigure his body. Jesus and Enoch also had physical bodies that they lived in perfectly, and so did not have to pass through death. They were literally able to transform and transfigure their bodies and raise them to a higher level of being. The teaching is that the great masters of the world can materialize and dematerialize their bodies at will, because they have completed that task of spiritualizing Earth.

It seems that Peter Deunov was once asked about the astrological chart of Jesus, whether it was full of trines and other favorable aspects. He replied that it was in fact full of squares and unfavorable aspects, because he had to overcome extraordinarily difficult challenges in his personal life, in order to accomplish such extraordinary work for humanity. I find it interesting that Jesus should have to work so profoundly with squares, for he came at a time when humanity had sunk to an all-time low in cruelty and oppression. It seems he took on the unenviable task of working to uplift humanity at its heaviest point of involvement in gross materiality.

How each pair moves to form its own "square."

In Part 1 partners move one behind the other, towards the center.
In Part 2 partners move side by side, Right shoulders towards the center.
In Part 3 partners move one behind the other, backs towards the center.
In Part 4 partners move side by side, Left shoulders towards the center.

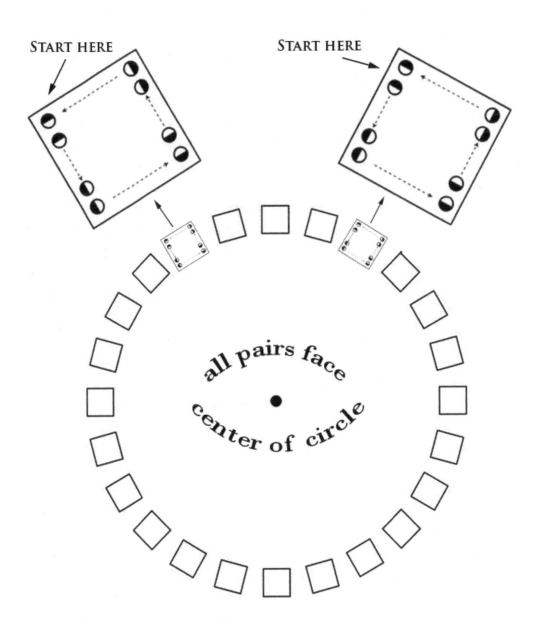

17. Description of Movements for Square: (64 bars)

Square is danced twice through in four parts:
Part 1: FACING the center of the circle, partners one behind the other.
Part 2: RIGHT shoulders towards the center, partners side by side.
Part 3: BACKS towards the center, partners one behind the other.
Part 4: LEFT shoulders towards the center, partners side by side.
Whole sequence (bars 1-16) is danced in each part, i.e. four times in all.
Whole dance sequence (Parts 1-4) then repeated from beginning to end.

Part 1: Facing the center: All make a quarter turn to the LEFT to face the center, partners one behind the other now in a double circle.

Starting Position: Feet together, hands pointing towards the heart and elbows out horizontally as in **Weaving**.

Bar 1: As in <u>diagram 17a</u>, Left knee bends as Right foot extends to the right and arms open out in a horizontal plane sideways, palms facing down.

Bar 2: Left leg straightens up as Right foot comes to join the left, while lower arms and hands swing horizontally back in front of the heart, fingers pointing towards each other, palms still down.

Bar 3: Right knee bends as Left foot extends to the left and arms swing out horizontally to the sides again.

Bar 4: Right knee straightens up as arms and Left foot return to starting position.

Bars 5-8: As in bars 1-4.

Bars 9-14: As in <u>diagram 17b</u>, palms face forward and, as the right foot steps forward, both arms swing up in two vertical arches and out to the horizontal, then, as the left foot steps forward, the arms swing up and round and back down to the heart. (Palms stay facing forward throughout the time we are walking forward towards the center.)

Bar 15: Pivoting a quarter turn to the LEFT on the left foot, the right foot swings round and steps, as the arms swing up and out. (Our Right shoulders are now towards the center of the circle.)

Bar 16: The left foot is placed alongside the right, while the arms come together again, (palms still facing forward.)

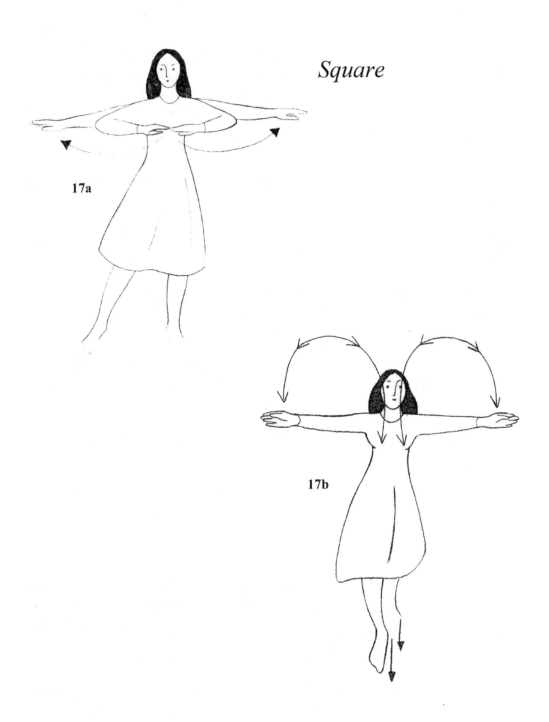

Square

17a

17b

Part 2: Right shoulders towards the center:

Forming now an inner circle, we repeat the whole sequence, Right shoulders towards the center of the circle. (In this quarter-segment of **Square**, we are facing and moving clockwise — the only place where we move clockwise in the PanEuRhythmy.)

Bars 17-30: As in bars 1-14, (but moving CLOCKWISE round the circle, RIGHT shoulders towards the center.)

Bars 31-32: As in bars 15-16, (all turning LEFT again, this time to face OUT from the circle, backs towards the center.)

Part 3: Backs towards the center:

We repeat the whole sequence again with our backs toward the center of the circle, (returning out to the outer circle.)

Bars 33-46: As in bars 1-14, (but moving and facing AWAY from the center.)

Bars 47-48: As in bars 15-16, (all turning LEFT again, this time to face COUNTER-CLOCKWISE round the circle.)

Part 4: Left shoulders towards the center:

We complete the square by again repeating the whole sequence, moving counterclockwise on the outer circle, (our left shoulders towards the center.)

Bars 49-62: As in bars 1-14, (but facing and moving COUNTER-CLOCKWISE round the circle, LEFT shoulders towards the center.)

Bars 63-64: As in bars 15-16, (all turning LEFT again to face the center as at the beginning.)

The whole sequence is then repeated from the beginning. We end this dance on the outer circle all facing the center, as we started.

18. Beauty

These next two movements have the same melody, which is interesting, because they have different rhythms. **Beauty** has a three-part rhythm, while that of **Flowing** has five parts. In these two movements, we are continuing the work of rising to the challenge of the "squares" in our life. In **Beauty** we are dancing a three-part rhythm to a five-part melody. This creates an interesting challenge, as we work on beautifying our life by invoking a subtler level of consciousness, the element of Air.

The element of Air is the element of mind. Subtle Air is the noosphere, literally: the sphere of mind. We need space, and we literally need air to think. Our minds will not work if we do not get enough oxygen to breathe. The element of Air is very important. The mind functions in Air and when we think, our eyes go out and up, as our consciousness moves out into space.

As we dance **Beauty,** we also spiritualize the element of Air. We spiritualize the element of Air by beautifying the thoughts in our minds. As human beings we are all working on this challenge of beautifying our minds, so that they can express the Divine realm of being — purifying our thoughts, filling our minds with positive thoughts, using affirmations, praying, connecting with the Divine, and so beautifying the subtle element of Air. Of course in this day and age we are faced with another challenge — to beautify and purify the gross element of Air as well, because at the moment we are polluting it so badly, that there is danger to all life on this planet.

In **Beauty**, we start with our right hand up. There are levels upon levels of meaning for this. **Beauty** is like a bird floating on the Air. We float and sway on the Air forward and backwards. Then we sweep our arm down, past our body and back, while bringing the other arm up and the other leg forward, swing round, and sway again forwards and backwards. As with **Aoum**, we move the leg and arm of the same side together. We feel the element of Air under our arms, as a bird floating through the currents of Air. We experience the beauty of the bird floating on the element of Air.

Beauty, along with Truth and Goodness, is one of the three essentials for life and growth. We nourish our souls on beauty, as we nourish our bodies with food. If we fill our minds with beauty, we contribute to the well-being of ourselves and all around us. Ugliness depresses and saps our energy. Beauty enlivens, uplifts and gives new life, hope, energy and vision, for "Without Vision, the people perish."

18. Description of Movements for Beauty: (90 bars)

Bar 1: Stepping onto the right foot, the right arm swings forward and up at a diagonal, while the left arm continues the line down and back, both palms down, left foot lifting slightly off the ground as one reaches forward.

Bar 2: Body rocks gracefully back, arms and hands resting lightly on the air like the wings of a bird, right foot lifting slightly off the ground.

Bar 3: Arms swinging past the sides of the body exchanging their relative positions, the body rocks forward again onto the right foot and the left leg swings forward.

Bar 4: Body steps forward onto the left foot, the left arm reaching forward and up, arms and hands resting on the air like a bird gliding, and making graceful, almost imperceptible little floating movements.

Bar 5: Body rocks back onto the right foot, arms still continuing their gliding motion.

Bar 6: Body sways forward again onto the left foot, while the arms swing past the sides of the body in opposite directions (returning to where they started,) and the right foot swings forward.

These movements are repeated gracefully and lightly to the end of the music.

19. Flowing

In **Flowing** we continue to work with the powerful challenges we started facing in **Square,** this time by harnessing the subtle element of Water, which is Love, the heart energy. We have set the scene by beautifying our mind with uplifting thoughts, and now we can empower our new thinking and consciousness by harnessing our heart energy into the work of transformation.

Let us look more closely at this subtle element of Water, which is Love. Water connects everything on the planet. Water connects all cells in a body together. Without water our cells would disintegrate and our bodies would not function. Similarly, water flows between all segments of earth and connects all together.

In C.S. Lewis' book, *Voyage to Venus,* the whole population of the planet lives on water. There is no solid ground. It is only when they have what they call "fixed land" that things start to go downhill, and evil appears. As long as they live on the Water element, on the floating islands, they keep their connection with the flow, the Love, the creative element and Divine plan.

Flowing is a very important part of our lives. As soon as we become rigid and stuck on the gross element of Earth, we become calcified and so completely caught up in matter that we fail to fulfill our Divine purpose. Mankind has to keep mobile and flexible, even on a physical level, because if we become arthritic or stiff, we cannot move. (I know this because at one time I had to cure myself of arthritis, in order to do my work with PanEuRhythmy!)

Flowing is internalizing the Love principle. When we are guided by Love, we flow. A rigid person is a person who is not guided by Love. If as a parent we are rigid, we are not truly loving our children. If I as a teacher become rigid, I am not truly loving my students. The qualities of the element of Water are extremely important on every level of life.

In this dance, we start, as in **Everá**, by connecting with the Stream of Love (through the feeling side of our nature) by stretching out our hands to the left. Then we turn around 180 degrees and give out that Love with outstretched arms to the world around us. As we do so, we find ourselves supported on the Ocean of Divine Love. Our arms float with the undulating movement of the waves, as we take three steps sideways, crossing one foot in front of the other on the second step.

Finally, as we turn and swing our hands together, we give that Love to ourselves also — the right (directing) hand caressing first the palm and then the back of the left (nurturing, supporting) hand, the inner masculine within us acknowledging the feminine within — before again swinging our arms out, (turning our attention 180 degrees out,) and finding ourselves once more floating on the Ocean of Divine Love.

Flowing
(as seen from inside the circle)

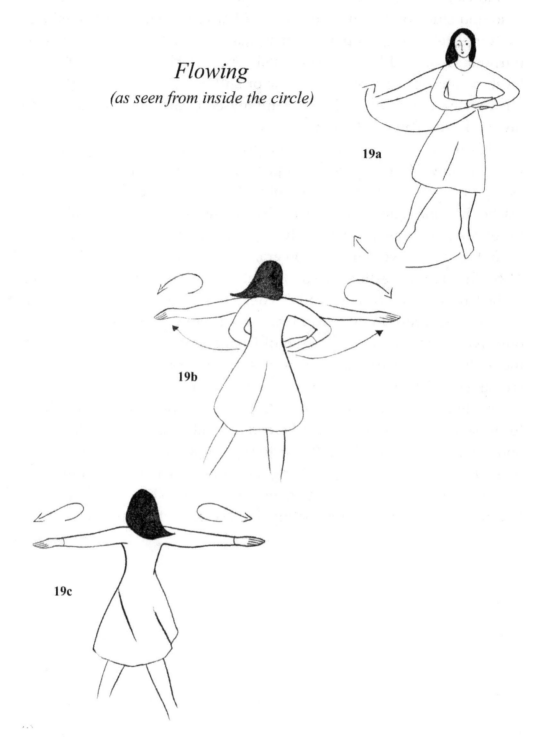

19a

19b

19c

19. Description of Movements for Flowing: (90 bars)

Starting position: Facing the center, hands together in front of the heart, (right palm above and caressing the left palm.)

Bar 1: <u>Diagram 19a:</u> We swing the body around on our right foot to face outwards from the center of the circle, the right palm caressing first the palm then the back of the left hand as it turns over.

Bar 2: <u>Diagram 19b:</u> With our backs to the center of the circle, our left foot steps out (in the counterclockwise direction of the circle), while our arms float out sideways from the body with the undulating movement of a wave.

Bar 3: <u>Diagram 19c:</u> Arms continue their undulating movement in rhythm with the music, as the Right foot crosses in front of the left leg and steps to the left.

Bar 4: Left leg extends out and steps to the left, arms still undulating to the music.

Bar 5: The body sways back onto the right foot, the hands swinging back together, (right palm over the left.)

Bar 6: While the right palm caresses first the palm, then the back of the left hand as it turns over, the body sways forward onto the left foot and swings round to face into the center again, the right leg swinging round the left.

Bar 7: As the right foot steps to the right, the arms float out sideways.

Bar 8: Left leg crosses in front of the right and steps to the right, the arms undulating to the sides in rhythm with each step.

Bar 9: Right leg extends to the right and steps, arms still undulating in wave-like motion.

Bar 10: Body sways back onto the left leg, and hands swing back together, (right palm over and caressing the left palm.)

These ten bars are repeated to the end of the music (90 bars)

20. Overcoming/Conquering

"Night-time is over!" says the Sun;
Sadness and fear are overcome.
Steadily forward we bravely press
Through days of happiness, through distress...

So press on, achieve your goal,
Fill with Light your hungry soul.
Heaven will help you on your way;
Love will cast all fear away.

Happy are they who see the track,
Never a thought of turning back,
Always of living for the Whole:
This is victory for the Soul."

These are the lyrics for the next movement, **Overcoming** or **Conquering** — a very fiery movement. Now we have faced the challenges of our "squares," we can move on to connect with the Fire in our Soul, which will enable us to overcome all obstacles in our lives.

The fourth element is Fire, and Fire is often associated with masculinity. There is a feminine Fire as well, but this dance is a very masculine dance. This movement strengthens our willpower and ability to overcome the obstacles of life.

In contrast to most of the other dances of the PanEuRhythmy, we do not move from side to side, (as we did in **Flowing**.) Rather we steadfastly face forward, remembering that the adversary in life is not somebody else, but whatever is holding us back from within. Even our shoulders stay resolutely facing forward, as our arms swing from side to side. So we keep our head, our shoulders, and our eyes unswervingly facing forward — fully focused on the goal as in Zen in the art of archery.

Overcoming starts even before the music starts — with our arms back to the right, symbolically drawing on the energy of Wisdom on the right. We could think of this as pulling back the string of a bow, before launching the arrow. The left knee is raised very deliberately and we bend forward from the waist slightly. In this Yin position, we are symbolically bowing to our opponent, expressing reverence as in the Eastern martial arts, and drawing in his energy, before moving forward to overcome. If we start with the thought in our minds: I am going to overcome, the heart follows, and we unleash the power of the Soul.

In **Overcoming** the palms are not so much used for healing as for overcoming or surmounting obstacles. If our obstacle is fear, for example, we have to get up and face it, because when we face it, we dissolve it.

As the music starts, we step on the left foot, then straighten up and step forward on the right foot, our arms swinging forward and up, palms very deliberately pushing forward. We then repeat the action the other way around, swinging our hands back down to the left, this time symbolically drawing on the energy of Divine Love, before moving forward again.

As we swing our arms up, and the palms turn to face forward, it is as if we are shining the light of our inner "projector" out into the world — making manifest on the "screen" of our life the inner vision and ideals from the "filmstrip" of our Souls.

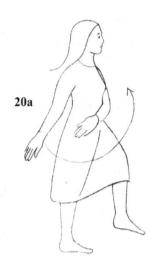

20a

Overcoming
(as seen from outside the circle)

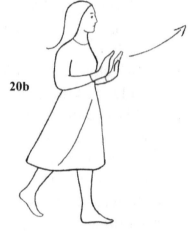

20b

20c

20. Description of Movements for Overcoming: (80 bars)

Starting position: <u>Diagram 20a:</u> Our arms are back to the right, both palms loosely facing the body slightly below the waist. Weight of the body is on the right foot, left knee is raised and left foot is off the ground, and we bend forward slightly from the waist.

Bar 1: <u>Diagram 20b:</u> Swinging the arms forward and up, we step onto our left foot, straightening up as we do so.

Bar 2: <u>Diagram 20c:</u> Stepping forward onto our right foot, our palms very deliberately push forward and up, the toes of the left foot almost leaving the ground behind us.

Bar 3: Swinging the arms back down to the left, our weight shifts back onto our left foot, and we raise the right knee, bending forward slightly as we do so.

Bar 4: Swinging the arms forward, we step onto our right foot, straightening up again.

Bar 5: Stepping forward onto the left foot, the hands again push forward and up, the toes of the right foot almost leaving the ground behind us.

Bar 6: Swinging the arms back down to the right, we sway back onto the right foot and raise the left knee, again bending forward slightly.

These six bars are repeated to the end of the music, ending with the right foot forward and the arms up on the last note, (as in bar 2.)

21. Joy of the Earth

Joy of the Earth is a very graceful and joyous dance. In each bar throughout the dance, the ankles are gracefully drawn towards one another, as little steps are made in the general forward direction of the dance. The wrists and hands meanwhile perform subtle rippling movements as if caressing the aura of the Earth.

Peter Deunov said that these hand movements imitate the undulating movements of the earth around the sun. In fact, the movements of the PanEuRhythmy generally are those of the celestial bodies in the universe, and that is one reason why so many people feel so comfortable and at home with them and with the music. I have heard innumerable people gasp with wonder after their first experience of dancing the Pan-EuRhythmy, saying that they felt they recognized it, as if they had known it long ago, though not, to their knowledge, in this life-time. Several have told me they felt they had known the music "in Heaven" before their birth. (See testimonial by Ana Orozco at the end of this Section.) One two-year-old listened with rapt attention to the music, and at the end pointed to the CD player, saying, "On! On!" insisting it be played again. Peter Deunov, when congratulated on this and other music, would always say, "I did not compose it. I merely give you what I hear in the Divine world."

There is great joy in this dance and it leads up to the next dance, **Acquainting,** where for the first time we link hands and look into the eyes of our partner. We have accomplished a great deal in our Spiritual evolution and made great progress. We are getting ready to begin to work in total harmony with others to build "Heaven on Earth" — the task for which we all know we were ultimately created.

We have now worked through four elements: Earth, Air, Water and Fire. The fifth element is Ether, an element that scientists used to say did not exist. However, the ancient scientists talked about ether, and in the tradition of India they call it Akasha. Today we talk about the Akashic records, because we have discovered that this fifth element does exist.

Ether is the substance of that subtle realm where everything exists, not only for a time but forever. When we utter a sound, it goes out into the element of Air, which is the element of mind. It goes out a certain distance, but as it goes out further from its source, it decreases in power and eventually disappears. Yet we are told nothing ultimately ever gets lost. The ripples I cause here go right round through the Ether to affect others on the other side of the planet. In the element of Air they do become lost, but in the element of Ether they are never lost. The Akashic records consist of the ripples that we put out, not only with our physical words, but subtly — through our thoughts and feelings. Everything that goes on within us creates ripples in the element of Ether, and those ripples go on forever.

People who can connect with the Akashic records can read the mind and feelings of people through all ages. This is very similar to how radio waves go out into space for ever and ever. We have proof; we have spaceships which send messages back even from beyond Saturn and Neptune. The element of ether is again being recognized. For a while it was too subtle for science to recognize, but science is now rediscovering the spiritual element as well. Nassim Haramein is going beyond Albert Einstein and demonstrating the unity of all levels of being, from the most dense material to the highest spiritual level.

Ether is that subtle element in which the creative sound of God begins to descend from the spiritual to the subtle realm, (the Akasha, the etheric level,) before it descends further into the gross physical level.

The first physical level is the level of air, which is invisible. We can feel it but not see it. Fire, Water, and Earth represent different degrees of subtlety down to gross materiality.

The element of Ether is the most purely spiritual element, and we reach it by purifying our thoughts and our feelings — all that we put out into the world. We are discovering more and more that what we put out on a subtle level comes back to us personally. That is why we are taught to think positively about everyone and everything, including ourselves, because even our thoughts have an effect.

If you have a project, if you have something you want to do, think about it positively. Write it out on a piece of paper. Do not show it to anybody, but keep it. The thought that you are putting out will gradually materialize, as you keep visualizing and affirming it positively, and working towards it.

We have talked about the symbolism of transmuting the subtle element of Ether, purifying, transforming, and spiritualizing that element. Let me now say a few things about the movement itself.

Joy of the Earth is a blessing of the Earth. When we have spiritualized and raised all the other four elements, then the Earth can also be in harmony with the subtler dimensions and become a paradise once more. Once we have spiritualized the four elements, we can have Heaven on Earth, and mankind can find, as Milton said, "Paradise regained," and so bless all that is, all Nature. The movement of **Joy of the Earth** is a blessing movement. We swing very gently and rhythmically from side to side, picking up our feet and progressing around the circle in little steps.

We swing our hands left and right, left and right, as if caressing the Earth's aura. I often visualize myself standing over a field of grain, just letting my hands skim over the ears of wheat like a deva blessing the crops. As we pass our hands to and fro in this way, we can feel the energy flowing through the palms of our hands, blessing the Earth.

As Homo sapiens, we have now entered our true vocation on planet Earth, and are conducting the symphony of life. In the Garden of Eden, Adam led the animals in an atmosphere of mutual love and harmony, and he gave them each a name. This function of naming is very important. Naming is giving identity, giving worth, giving respect, giving a function to all that is. So naming the different forms of creation is blessing and giving them each a function. Like the conductor who in turn calls up the strings, the woodwind, and the percussion, so man as a conductor of the physical world is calling up the different parts of the orchestra, and bringing them all into play in a harmonious and concerted way. As the conductor who is conducting the orchestra, in this dance we are blessing and conducting, performing our true functions as human beings, directing all towards truth.

Animals will naturally follow human beings who love them, because they respect man's higher consciousness. The animal world is suffering because man is not giving them love and direction. A true master will love and direct an animal, and that animal will be devoted, not only for life, but beyond one lifetime, to that human being.

There is a beautiful account in Richard Bach's book, *A Bridge Across Forever*, of how, when Richard and Leslie were practicing leaving and re-entering their bodies at will, they saw another spiritual body in their room, and recognized with great joy their beloved cat which had died a few years before, and were delighted to be reunited with her! Then they saw the silver cord from the spiritual form of their cat going down to a sleeping cat in a basket. When they looked at the silver cord, they noticed that the silver cord was connected with the cat that lived with them now! So they realized that the cat whose subtle body they had recognised, when they were out of their bodies, had returned to them in the form of their present cat.

An animal will love beyond death, and will return to its owners. The devotion of an animal is quite incredible, to a master who is truly human. I have been deeply touched by stories of some of the great spiritual men of India, who go out into the Himalayas or the jungle. For instance, a great saint of India, Sadhu Sundhar Singh, would go out and a leopard would come up to him and even nuzzle his neck against him. People who can make friends with lions and tigers are deeply spiritual people. They do not eat the flesh of animals. They love and respect the animals, and the animals recognize and follow them. At the moment, mankind is doing the opposite — terrorizing and exploiting the animal world, by misusing our superior power and superior consciousness.

Joy of the Earth celebrates the time when the whole earth will rediscover the joy for which it was created, and the song of the angels,

"Peace on earth, goodwill towards all," will at last become a reality. Then the animal world and the plant world will once again be able to respect and love their human cousins. When the earth returns to being a paradise, *"the wolf shall dwell with the lamb; and the calf and the young lion together; and a little child shall lead them."* (Isaiah 11:6)

As a child, those words from Isaiah always touched me deeply, though, in the aftermath of World War 2, they seemed almost impossibly idealistic. Yet they always resonated in my heart. Now it moves me to tears to see how they are actually beginning to come true in the world today — with the prayers of so many and the quiet, dedicated work of the United Nations and other peace-loving groups.

"They shall beat their swords into plowshares and their spears into pruning hooks: nation shall not lift up sword against nation, neither shall they learn war any more." (Isaiah 2:4) *"They shall not hurt nor destroy.... for the earth shall be filled with the knowledge of God, as the waters cover the sea."* (Isaiah 11:9)

21. Description of Movements for Joy of the Earth:
(80 bars)

In each bar of the dance, the ankles are gracefully drawn towards one another, and little steps are made in the general counter-clockwise direction of the dance. The wrists and hands meanwhile perform subtle rippling movements as if caressing the aura of the Earth.

Starting Position: <u>Diagram 21a:</u> Facing the center, (partners one behind the other,) feet apart and arms to the Right, palms down, weight of the body on the Right foot, left toes extended and just touching the ground.

Bar 1: Weight of the body swings onto the Left foot, the Right foot lifting gently from the ground, its ankle gracefully moving towards, but not touching, the left ankle. Both palms, facing down and gently extended in front, sweep across to the Left, making soft little undulations like the wind rippling over a field of grass.

Bar 2: The Right foot extends itself forward in a little step to the Right, and the Left foot, its ankle moving gracefully towards the Right, comes closer to the right foot. Meanwhile the arms and body sway to the Right, the hands still making subtle little rippling movements.

Joy of the Earth
(as seen from inside the circle)

21a

21b

21c

2x each way

2x each way

Bar 3: As Bar 1.

Bar 4: As Bar 2, but the Left foot lifts, as the whole body starts turning to the right.

Bar 5: <u>Diagram 21b:</u> With the weight of the body on the Right foot, the hands lift up in front of the heart and the palms turn to face one another. Simultaneously the Left foot swings past the Right and steps forward in the general direction of the dance, the arms reaching forward and up (as in "Everá,") and the body completes its turn to the Right, right toes extended back.

With our backs to the center, these movements are repeated in the next five bars with all the steps inverted, as follows. (Throughout the dance, the ankles are gracefully drawn towards one another and the hands continue their rippling movements of caressing the Earth's aura.)

Bar 6: <u>Diagram 21c:</u> With our backs now to the center we face out. Our arms swing down and back to the Right, the weight of the body shifting onto the Right foot.

Bar 7: The arms swing forward again to the Left, weight of the body shifting onto the Left foot.

Bar 8: The arms swing back to the Right, weight of the body shifting onto the Right foot.

Bar 9: The arms swing forward to the Left and towards the heart, and the Right foot begins to move past the Left.

Bar 10: The Right foot steps forward and the whole body completes its swing around to the Left, while the arms extend forward and up in the general direction of the dance, (as in Bar 5, but with opposite feet.)

These ten bars are repeated to the end of the dance, alternately (every five bars) facing the center or facing out from the circle. (80 bars)

What Paneurhythmy means to me

"When I first learnt Paneurhythmy
it seemed to be just another step in my spiritual exploration,
but when I started practicing Paneurhythmy,
it turned out to be a miraculous way of exploring myself.
It instantly became a meaningful part of my life
and part of myself.
Dancing Paneurhythmy enabled me
to discover so much about myself
that I had previously not experienced.
Thanks to Paneurhythmy I found answers
and solutions to "issues" I had been concerned about
which had previously seemed impossible to resolve.

When I started dancing together with my friend,
Paneurhythmy revealed another wonderful dimension.
We experienced great energy of places and people,
and I realized that the more people dance Paneurhythmy,
the more powerful it becomes.
This was particularly true in the Rila mountains
where I had the opportunity to dance
in the place where Paneurhythmy was born.
It was magnificent!
Today I can say that Paneurhythmy has helped me
find God, love and joy.
It has become my way of life,
my thankful prayer and understanding of life –
everything is just as it should be."

Lidia Klimowicz, Poland, 2009
(Co-ordinating teacher of PanEuRhythmy in Poland)

Section 4

Working in Partnership

The next five dances of the PanEuRhythmy are dances of Partnership. They represent that stage in our spiritual evolution when we are mature enough to work in perfect harmony with another being to accomplish the task of bringing on earth the Kingdom of Heaven or, to quote the poet Milton, "Paradise regained."

The dances progress through the stages of partnership that we often associate with marriage, that most challenging of all partnerships: from the joyful exhilaration of the early stages of becoming acquainted; through the commitment to step out together and link and harmonize at every level of our being; through the rapturous moments of celebrating how happy we are that the partnership is working out; on through the long haul of persevering through all difficult and arid parts of our journey together; until we reach the grand finale of our triumphant Homecoming, acclaimed by the host of unseen witnesses cheering us on and waiting to receive us into the subtler realms of being awaiting us on completion of our life's pilgrimage.

22. Acquainting/Friendship

"Touch of a hand is blessing a friend.
Through friendship and love our souls will blend.
Lighter our burden grows when, with a friend so close,
Feelings and thoughts so high meet eye to eye.
Blessings abundant flow through every soul.
We feel the Hand Divine making us whole."

As so eloquently expressed in its lyrics, this dance, **Acquainting,** beautifully expresses the quality of relating to others in love, and how the love we share is part of the greater Divine Love radiating out through the world.

We start by holding hands with our partner and, looking into each other's eyes, we recognize and respond to that Divine essence shining through our partner's eyes, the windows of their soul. We then let go our partner's hands, as we raise our eyes heavenwards in thankfulness, briefly touching our own heart center, before flinging open our arms and our hearts in gratitude to the heavens for the joy of acquainting with another such wonderful being, and sharing our love and joy with all. Finally, we bring our hands back together, clasping our own palms and feeling the Love circling within our own being, before turning again to share with our partner the love and joy deep in our own heart.

These three movements together express the ongoing sharing of Love, (with the partner, with the Universe and with one's own self.) The energy passes down from the heart through the right arm, and is received into the partner's heart through the left hand and arm. First we link hands with our partner to form with them a circuit of energy moving from our partner up our left arm and through our heart, then down our right arm towards our partner again. Next we let go our partner's hands to allow this circuit of Love to flow out freely through the whole Universe, where, as Einstein discovered, all straight lines ultimately become circles. So the love we have freely given finally returns to us, and we realize the oneness of that love-energy flowing through all that is. Finally, clasping our own hands together, we experience that circuit of love and joy flowing through our own being and the fullness of our own self-love, out of which we can then return in love to our partner — and again experience together the flow of Divine Love and Joy.

This dance follows on naturally from the last five, for, when we have fulfilled our function of guiding and directing appropriately all levels of nature, the animal and the plant kingdoms, and are in tune with the angelic realms, we can at last find one another in Paradise, and move on together to enact in perfect harmony the Divine plan of creating Heaven on Earth.

These last five dances are some of the most beautiful and form the culmination of the PanEuRhythmy. It is interesting and perhaps significant that the first of these dances is #22, which in Numerology represents a high degree of Mastery. Symbolically we have now reached the point in our spiritual evolution where we have attained a high enough degree of self-mastery that we can enter into a very fine quality of partnership. Up till now we have been dancing side-by-side, each working on our own evolution, being aware of our partner but not connecting directly. Now, for the first time, we turn to face our partner, for only now are we ready to really acquaint ourselves with each other.

We have worked through these wonderful stages of bringing back the Kingdom of Heaven on earth, recreating the Garden of Eden, Paradise on Earth, so now we can move on to work with others in partnership and get to know one another as truly Divine beings. We have risen to our full stature, to the high calling of each one of us, knowing that each of us is not just an isolated little human being, but a very great soul incarnate.

In India somebody who is truly manifesting his greatness of Soul is called *Mahatma*. *Maha* means great, and *atma* means spirit or soul. *Atma* comes from the word for breathing, *(atmen* in German,) because Spirit is the breath of life. So somebody who truly realizes his soul's potential is a Great Soul or Spirit. Gandhi was called Mahatma Gandhi, because he was truly living out his Divine purpose. This dance expresses the joy of discovering someone else who is also living out his or her Divine purpose. The extraordinary joy of meeting and working with such a person is truly magnificent and inspirational.

22. Description of Movements for Acquainting: (60 bars)
Starting Position: Partners turn to face each other, (one partner facing outward in the circle and the other inward.) Clasping both of our partner's hands, (Right palms over Left,) we look into each other's eyes.
Bar 1: Diagram 22a: We swing together forward in the general direction of the dance, the weight of the body rocking onto the forward foot, and our eyes moving out and up in thanksgiving to the Universe.
Bar 2: Diagram 22b: Our bodies continue forward, pivoting out 180-degrees on the forward foot, while the one behind sweeps past to step in front. As our bodies turn away from one another, we let go hands and our arms sweep out from the heart, as if flinging open wide the gates of the heart. (Partners are now back to back, our arms wide open welcoming all of life, and our eyes looking out and up in thanksgiving.)
Bar 3: While still back to back, we both rock back onto our back foot, and our forward hand sweeps back into the palm of the hand further back, (Right palm over Left in both cases.)
Bar 4: Diagram 22c: Still holding our own hands together, we swing forward and round, pivoting 180-degrees on our forward feet, till we face each other again and can transfer our palms into each others' hands, (still Right palms over Left, so our hands do not need to turn over.)

Acquainting

(as seen from inside the circle)

22a

22b

22c

Bar 5: Looking into each other's eyes, the partners together swing further FORWARD, (NOT back!) the weight of our bodies transferring onto our forward feet.

Bar 6: Still looking into each other's eyes, we finally swing back together, the weight of the body rocking back onto the back foot.

These six movements are repeated in each set of six bars to the end of the music.

23. Beautiful Day

In this second of the Partnership dances, the focus is on Balance at all levels of our being. In **Acquainting**, we connected for the first time with our partners directly. And this is a little like falling in love. You look at the person and realize what a Divine, splendid, wonderful being is in your partner. And you see that Light in their eyes and you feel a heart connection with them. And then you turn out and open wide the portals of your heart, opening to the whole world and sharing that Light and that Love.

In this dance, as we move into a **Beautiful Day**, we are practicing balance within our own being as well as in our shared work with our partner, so that we can together create a beautiful day. The leg movements are very subtle and delicate, for we are embarking on a delicate enterprise — as we all know from our experiences of entering into new partnerships. The challenge throughout this dance is balance. We not only stand on one foot at a time for several moments, but we also flex the knee and bob up and down on that same leg, while holding the other foot off the ground. We have to focus and remain quiet within, in order to accomplish this with grace and poise.

This dance is in four parts. We begin with our hands on our hips because the focus is on our lower body and lower chakras, getting them into harmony and balance. We raise the right knee and, standing on the left leg and bending the left knee, we bounce down and up three times on the left leg before stepping down onto the right foot. We are finding that delicate balance within our own being. In order to keep the right knee up, the right leg relaxed, and bend with the left knee, one has to be in a subtle inner state of balance.

In the second part of the dance we extend that balance to the upper body and upper chakras, by including the arms in the movement. For the first part of the dance we were just using our legs. Now we also use our arms. We raise our right hand along with our right knee, and balance on the left leg, with the right hand and the right knee raised. The feeling side of our nature is supporting and balancing, giving that little bounce, that little rhythm to allow the thinking side of our nature to really manifest in the world. And then the right hand swings down and the left hand swings up along with the left knee, and we balance this time on the right leg. In this second part of the dance, we are still working on establishing balance within our own being and are not yet actually holding hands with our partner.

Only in the third part of the dance do we physically connect with our partner. We take hold of our partner's hand, the right hand over the left, (because the left hand is the supportive or receiving hand and the right hand the giving hand.) The outer hand is on our hip and now, in harmony and in rhythm with our partner, we balance on the left leg and raise the right knee and, with the toes of the right foot just above the ground, bounce three times on the left leg, before stepping down onto the right foot. We then repeat these movements, this time with our left knee raised.

The PanEuRhythmy up to now has been bringing us into balance as individuals. Now, in partnership, we're learning to find that same inner balance, first on the left leg and then on the right leg. As the left leg symbolizes our feeling nature and the right leg our thinking nature, we are also finding that inner balance between our thinking and our feeling natures, first within our own being and then within the partnership.

As well as working on creating something beautiful for God in our own lives, we are now also doing it together with our partner. We become aware of the delicate connection in the partnership, as we need to be inwardly poised, both in our own inner balance and in the mutual balance with our partner.

The balance between the two partners becomes even more delicate in the fourth sequence, as our outer arms now sweep up and over our heads to link hands with our partner. This movement of the arms can be very majestic and graceful. As the right feet step forward, the outer arms sweep out from the body and up, arching high as a Gothic arch over our heads to connect with our partner's outer hand. Meanwhile, the inner hands let go — symbolizing letting go of our need to hold on to each other for support, and trusting that the Universe will support us as we together create this Gothic beauty.

Then as our left feet move forward, we let go of our outer hands clasped over our heads, stretching our arms up and out as they gracefully swing down to our (outer) sides again, while our inner hands connect again, and, bending our elbows, we bring our hands up to shoulder level — symbolically forming again that physical connection between us, which balances and strengthens the outer spiritual endeavor we are engaged in together.

In this fourth sequence the outer partners lift their right arms and right legs together, a more masculine movement since the whole body moves together — first the right arm and leg rising together, then the left arm and leg together. The inner partners lift their left (outer) arms along with their right legs, the upper and lower body turning in opposite directions and pivoting at the waist — a more feminine movement, as women move more from the waist.

As the music comes to an end, our feet come together, and we continue to hold hands above our heads for just a moment longer, before releasing them out sideways again — slowly and gracefully in a downward arching movement. When performed with poise and grace, this is a very beautiful movement, symbolizing the beauty of a truly harmonious partnership in a great enterprise.

23. Description of Movements for Beautiful Day:

(144 or 112 bars) Music is in two parts, which alternate.

This majestic, stately dance is danced in pairs like a court dance, requiring careful coordination in order to maintain balance. We hold our bodies tall and upright throughout, taking only one very small step forward every four bars. The arm movements change in each of the four Parts, whereas **the dipping leg movements continue unchanging throughout.**

PART 1: (32 bars.) **This sequence of eight bar-movements is repeated four times**, as the **first** part of the music is played:

Starting position: Standing tall in pairs, facing in the general counter-clockwise direction of the dance, hands on hips, thumbs back. Weight of the body is on the Left foot, Right knee is raised, toes dropping loosely down.

Bars 1-3: Diagram 23a: Standing tall and elegant, we bend and then straighten the Left (supporting) knee/leg in each bar, causing the whole body to dip down and up again.

Bar 4: We step onto the Right foot, stepping only slightly forward as we do so, and raise the Left knee.

Bars 5-7: With the Left knee raised, the dipping movements continue on the Right leg.

Bar 8: Stepping now onto the Left foot, we raise the Right knee.

Beautiful Day

23a

23b

23c

23d

PART 2: (24 bars.) **This sequence of eight bar-movements is repeated three times**, as the **second** part of the music is played.
The dipping movement of the body continues, as the supporting leg flexes and straightens in each bar. In addition, **Diagram 23b**, alternating with the feet every four bars, one hand is raised, palm forward as in a salutation.

Bar 33: With the Right knee raised and Right hand held up, palm facing forward as in salutation, we dip down and up again on the Left leg.

Bars 34/5: Left leg flexes in each bar, as Right hand and knee stay up.
Bar 36: Left leg continues to flex, as the Right foot steps down, and the Right hand returns to its original position on the right hip.

Bar 37: The Left knee and hand are raised, palm again facing forward, while the Right leg takes over the dipping movement.

Bars 38/9: As in bars 34/5, but the other way round.
Bar 40: As the Left foot steps down, the Left hand returns to the left hip.

PART 3: (32 bars) **Diagram 23c:**
The **first** part of the music is repeated from the beginning (as in Part 1), and the leg movements continue as in the previous two Parts. Throughout Part 3, the partners clasp inner hands at about shoulder level, right palm down and left palm up, while the outer hands rest on our hips.

PART 4: (56 bars or 24 bars) The **second** part of the music is played, followed normally by the **first** part for the third and last time, though this is sometimes omitted. **This sequence of eight bar-movements is repeated seven times, to the second and then the first part of the music** — three times only when the first part of the music is not repeated.

Bar 1: Diagram 23d: Left knees bend and straighten as Right knees are raised, and partners swing their OUTER arms out sideways and up and over their heads and clasp hands, forming an arch together. (Left hand is turned palm up, and Right palm down.) Inner hands are unclasped and lowered.

Bars 2 and 3: The outer hands remain clasped, while the Left knees flex and then straighten in each bar.

Bar 4: Right feet step forward, and outer hands unclasp and swing up and out and down again, until the outer arms rest loosely down our outer sides. At the same time the Left knees and inner forearms are raised, and we clasp inner hands, as in the previous PART 3.

Bars 5-7: The inner hands remain clasped at the level of the shoulders, and the dipping movement is repeated three times with the Right legs.

Bar 8: As the Left feet step down, the inner hands unclasp and drop down by our sides, while the outer arms swing out and up and over our heads, to clasp hands again as in Bar 1 of PART 4.
At the end we stand still a moment with hands clapsed above our heads, before gracefully arching back out and down again.

24. How Happy We Are!

In this, the third of the five partnership dances, we are celebrating how happy we are that our partnership is working. And globally humanity is gradually learning that it is much more pleasant and healthy for all concerned if we can communicate with love and in harmony.

This dance **How Happy We Are!** is based on an old Bulgarian courtship dance, "Ratshenitsa," which was in a minor key. As a result of the Bulgarians being oppressed by the Turks for five hundred years, their music tended to have a sad, nostalgic tone. Peter Deunov said it was very important to change this sadness into joy and to let go of suffering. We have been through centuries of suffering, and suffering, he said, has been our main teacher, but now we are moving out of the age of suffering. We can be thankful for the suffering we have been through and let it go. Suffering has been like a scourge, the stick that has woken up the donkey and gotten us moving, but we don't have to hold onto it any more. Now that we are awake and our hearts are opening to Love, we can respond and let Love be our teacher.

We are moving forward into a new age of harmony and joy. We can see this in the world all around us at the moment. In South Africa the blacks and the whites are forgiving the past, working together and governing themselves together. The Israelis and the Arabs are working to find ways to live together. In Northern Ireland Catholics and Protestants are overcoming their differences. Russians come "from Russia with love," and now so many Americans are going, with love, over to Russia. This is also happening in Poland, in Vietnam, in Latin America and between so many peoples who have been at war in the past, though we may not always hear about such initiatives on the media. Nonviolent Communication and the Nonviolent Peaceforce are helping people to resolve their differences harmoniously, while so many UN and other initiatives are facilitating efforts to rebuild societies torn by war and global exploitation. We are living in an exciting time, when the conflicted peoples of the world are making efforts to come together in love and harmony. We are learning to find a new harmony together, and that is what we are celebrating in this dance.

This is a very light, springing dance in which the heels almost never touch the ground. On each step we bounce twice, as a way of expressing the love and joy that we are feeling. We start with our hands on our hips and, bouncing twice on each step, we take three steps forward and rock back on our left foot for the fourth step. For every few steps forward in life, it is normal and natural to take a step back. We make a few steps and progress forward in our lives, then we have to go back and recap or re-evaluate ourselves, to strengthen where we have come from.

After the fourth sequence of four steps, there is a new sequence. We let our arms swing loosely down, take our partner's hand, and while taking two steps forward, we together swing both hands forward and up. Then as we take a step back, we swing both arms down and back. This sequence is repeated almost six times.

As we are coming to the end of the sixth time, we release our partner's hand, put our hands on our hips again, and repeat the first sequence of three bouncing steps forward and one back. These two sequences are repeated alternately to the end of the music, which is normally played through twice. However, it is such an enjoyable dance that sometimes the musicians play extra music, so that we can dance the two sequences through seven times in all.

As mentioned in the chapter on **Clapping**, the words "Grace" and "Gratitude" both come from the same Latin root. A heart filled with gratitude attracts Divine grace. When we can be grateful for everything in life, Spiritual progress is rapid. The key is to be grateful for whatever comes our way, even trauma and suffering. When somebody hurts us and we respond by thanking that person or thanking the Universe for that suffering, we have found the "nutcracker" that will crack open the hard rough "shell" of suffering and release the kernel of blessing hidden within it. "Welcoming every event as an advent" transforms life into a Spiritual adventure.

This zestful and exhilarating dance helps us to throw ourselves joyfully and whole-heartedly into life, so that we can find ourselves truly being thankful and celebrating "How happy we are!"

24. Description of Movements for How Happy We Are!
(32 bars repeated 2 or 7 times.)

This is a very light, springing dance in which the heels need hardly ever touch the ground...

PART 1: (16 bars) Hands on our hips throughout, this four-step movement (three steps forward and one back) is repeated four times.

Starting Position: Diagram 24a: In pairs facing counter-clockwise round the circle, hands on our hips, thumbs at the back.

Bar 1: We step and then bounce on the Right foot, Left foot gently raised to the back.
Bar 2: We step and then bounce on the Left foot, Right foot gently raised to the back.
Bar 3: We step and then bounce on the Right foot, left foot gently raised to the back.
Bar 4: We rock back onto our Left foot and then bounce, the Right leg gently raised in front.

These four bars are repeated four times. In the last bar we swing both our arms down and back in readiness for PART 2.

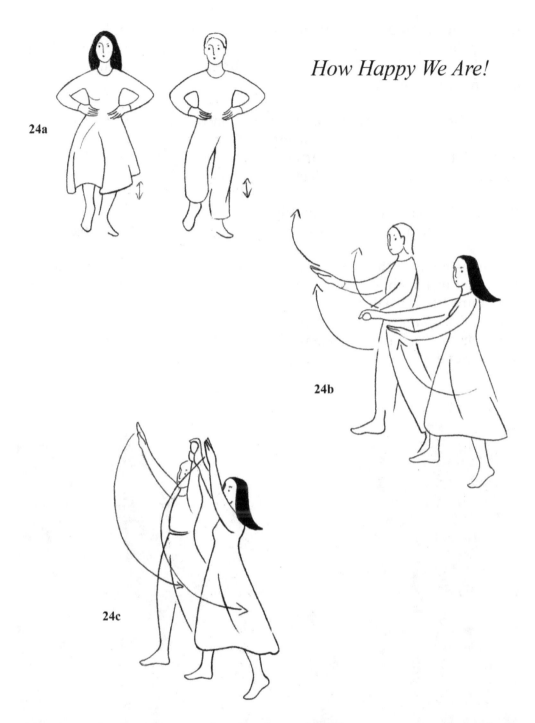

How Happy We Are!

24a

24b

24c

PART 2: (16 bars) Inner hands clasped with our partner throughout, **both arms** swing loosely and freely in a three-step movement (forward, up, down,) repeated five times and with an extra forward movement at the end.

Bar 1: <u>Diagram 24b:</u> Clasping our partner's nearest hand throughout, we step forward onto the Right foot, swinging both arms forward and towards the shoulders, bending at the elbows as we do so, lightly lifting the Left foot up behind.

Bar 2: <u>Diagram 24c:</u> We step forward on the Left foot, lifting up the Right foot lightly behind, and swing both arms forward and with a light push all the way up, both arms outstretched, palms of outer hands opening towards the front, still clasping inner hands.

Bar 3: We rock back onto our Right foot, lifting the Left leg gently in front and swinging both our arms loosely all the way down and back.

The movements of these three bars are repeated five times, (with the Left and Right feet leading alternately.) In the 16th (and last) bar, as we rock back onto the leg behind we let go our partner's hand and both hands swing back onto our hips in readiness for Part 1 again, (except in the final bar of the dance, when we keep hold of our partner's hand and together end with a jubilant swing forward and up.)

25. Step by Step

The fourth dance in the Partnership series is called **Step by Step**. This dance is teaching us about the step by step process of completing the long journey of life. We have experienced the joy of getting to know each other, then the exhilaration of the honeymoon, and now we have to move on, taking life step by step by being "in the here and now." There are times of rejoicing when we see the big vision, but we can only accomplish the vision when we live it out step by step. It's not that we've "bitten off more than we can chew." "You can eat an elephant, but only one bite at a time." So in this movement we learn to be very centered and take life "step by step."

Peter Deunov said that in this dance we are strengthening our nervous system. We are finding an inward strength and centeredness within our being. We are conducting solar energies into the earth and earth energies back up to the sun. Our bodies are like trees, conducting the energies of Heaven and Earth so that a blending can take place. This is the function of human beings and also of trees. As step out, we open up to the solar energies, directing them into the earth, and when our feet come together we are connecting with the energies of the earth and directing them heavenward.

The music in this dance is very picturesque. It has a soulful quality, like the soul's yearning for our heavenly home, wanting to complete our pilgrimage, to complete what we came into this world to do. We are wanting to perfect the picture we came to paint or the statue we came to sculpt in this world. And we have to go at it step by step. If a sculptor is for one moment distracted, he can chip the wrong bit off the block, and then the whole statue is destroyed. So in life we have to go step by step. It is so easy to chip off the wrong part of the statue. With our lives we are sculpting this beautiful gift that we are leaving to the world, and we want to have it perfect and complete. So we have to bring full attention to every detail, every step.

The music has a soulful, yearning, dancing quality, as if our heart and soul are dancing with the angels, yet our feet have to connect with the ground. Sometimes I find that one can be so entranced by the music that it is very easy to lose our place in the dance. This serves as a constant reminder to stay grounded, to stay with the movement of our feet, even while our soul is listening to the heavenly music, to keep our connection both with the heavenly music and with the Earth.

In this dance we are reminded of the interdependence of an orchestra. The bass and the percussion, by keeping the rhythm going, bring out more fully the beautiful melodies of the violins, the oboes, the flutes, and so on. Whatever instrument you're playing in the orchestra, you have to listen to all the others as well. The same applies to ourselves; whether our consciousness is in our soul, or in our eyes, ears, or feet, we have to also keep it in the moment. It's a matter of staying aware of the two extremities; it's important to be grounded, but it's also important to listen to the "distant drummer," to hear the heavenly music inspired by the heavenly vision. Otherwise, as the saying goes, "without Vision, the people perish." Unless we have that heavenly vision, life loses its meaning and purpose, and we get depressed or disoriented and lose our strength and direction. We have to keep our eye on the heavenly goal, our ears attuned to the heavenly music, and also have our feet firmly on the ground. This is the challenge of human life, if we are going to live it to the fullest.

As we dance we keep our eyes forward and up, at least horizontal or a little higher. It is not necessary to look at our feet because, as the Native Americans say, we do have "eyes in our feet" or "eyes in the tips of our toes." These "eyes in the tips of our toes" are the eyes of the body and can see the way forward, so we can allow the lower part of the body to find its own way. The eyes in the head are the windows of the Soul and need to keep the Vision in sight and the ears listening to the heavenly music. As we dance let us take in the feast of Nature around us. With our ears we take in the singing of the birds, the sound of the breeze rustling through the trees, and the sound of the Silence permeating all space. We take in the sights and sounds of Nature, because our spirits need to be fed from a higher source, while our feet are doing their work on the ground. This, in a way, is a parable of Life. We need to constantly allow our souls to be fed from above, to keep open to the heavenly manna, so that with the physical part of our being we can carry out our part in the Divine plan on Earth.

Step by Step is a little like "court dancing." We move tall and stately and avoid looking at our feet. In these last few dances we do a lot with the feet, and it's very easy to keep looking down, but it's important to keep our head up, our eyes looking forward and up, and remember that our feet can look after themselves.

We need to keep the feet relaxed and move with the thighs, allowing the lower leg and foot to drop to the ground in a very easy way — toes connecting first and feeling out the ground, before we touch the ground with the ball of the foot, then the heel, and shift the weight of the body by degrees onto that foot. Part of our consciousness knows exactly what our feet are doing without our eyes having to check on them. By doing this we are expanding our vision and opening beyond what the physical eyes can see, thereby increasing our peripheral vision.

In truth what you are doing is slipping out of physical seeing into clairvoyant seeing, the super-sensory seeing, because there's a sense in which, if you can really open up your vision, you can see all around you, even behind, above, and below. People who are clairvoyant say that clairvoyance usually comes with the peripheral vision. As soon as they look directly at, say, an angel or a fairy, they don't see it any more. They only see them out of the corner of their eye. People who see auras don't look directly at the person. They look to one side, and then they see the person's aura with their peripheral vision. In **Step by Step** we are expanding our consciousness in all directions — up, down, all around and from the lowest to the highest planes of consciousness.

Step by Step

25a

25b

25c

25d

25. Description of Movements for Step by Step: (88 bars)

Step by Step calls for great precision and focused attention. We remain centered and inwardly still, without bouncing as in the previous dance.

The steps of this dance are also in marked contrast to the music which is very interesting and varied. One can enjoy the music, but should avoid being too engrossed in it, as it is easy to lose one's place in the dance. Here, as in other places in the music, there are little tests, moments which serve as touchstones for our being present and consciously alert!

The hands stay on the hips throughout, and only the feet move. Except when stepping forward, the weight of the body stays on the supporting leg which remains straight throughout and does NOT bend, (in contrast to the other similar movements, like **Square.**)

Starting Position: All stand facing in the general counter-clockwise direction of the dance, feet together, hands on hips, thumbs back.

Bar 1: **Diagram 25a:** RIGHT leg bends and extends gracefully to the RIGHT, toes delicately touching the ground, then lifts again and returns to the Left foot. (Weight of the body stays on Left leg which remains straight.)
Bar 2: As in bar 1.

Bar 3: **Diagram 25b:** RIGHT leg lifts and extends FORWARD, toes just touching the ground, then returns to its place next to the Left foot. Weight of the body stays on the Left leg which does not move or bend.
Bar 4: As in bar 3.

Bar 5: Right foot steps forward, then Left foot steps forward.
Bar 6: Right foot steps forward, then Left foot steps beside the right.

Bar 7: **Diagram 25c:** LEFT leg lifts and extends to the LEFT, toes just touching the ground, then lifts again and returns to the Right foot. (Weight of the body stays on the Right leg which does not move or bend.)
Bar 8: As in bar 7.

Bar 9: **Diagram 25d:** LEFT leg lifts and extends FORWARD, toes just touching the ground, then returns to its place next to the Right foot. (Weight of the body stays on the Right leg which does not move or bend.)
Bar 10: As in bar 9.

Bar 11: LEFT foot steps forward, then RIGHT foot.
Bar 12: LEFT foot steps forward, then Right foot steps beside Left foot.

These twelve bars repeat without variation throughout.

26. At Dawn

This dance is like a grand finale. We've done the journey through life, we've almost crossed the desert, and we're now coming to the promised land. As we come into the promised land it's like the end of one lifetime or one life cycle. Many people, when dying or moving on in some way, get that sense of the invisible cloud — or crowd — of witnesses who are applauding and leading us on. There is a story in the Bible of the children of Israel once feeling totally overwhelmed by the enemy, because they were few in number and they were surrounded by hundreds of their enemies. They thought that they were going to be defeated. The prophet prayed and the voice of an angel said, "Look around you. Those who are with you are far more in number than those who are against you." When the prophet opened his eyes and looked around, all around them he saw hundreds and hundreds of angels, all armed with flaming swords. Suddenly he realized that there was no way they could lose the battle. And sure enough, even though they were only a small group, they won.

That, in a way, is a parable for what is happening in our lives. There are times in our lives when we feel overwhelmed by tremendous odds.

When the darkness seems overwhelming, let us remember that vision of the prophet, that those of the Light who are with us are far greater than those who are against us. We all have physical, material problems in our lives, but actually the hosts of angels, the hosts of unseen witnesses around us, far outnumber the physical problems. Though we may think we're at the end of our resources, we're not. These heavenly hosts can regenerate our body and energy so that we're able to move on to a higher level of being, and soon it will feel like a new day is dawning.

This dance is in three parts. In the first part, with our hands on our hips we swing one leg around the other, then take four steps forward, finishing with the feet together. These circling foot movements build up the magnetism in our being, strengthening and protecting us with the energy of Nature and the earth which is at its freshest and most powerful at dawn.

In the second part of the dance, we hold inner hands with our partner, swinging back and forwards, shifting our weight onto our heels, then onto our toes. As we know from Reflexology, we can work on every part of the body through the feet. The various organs of the lower part of the body each have their center in the heel, those of the waist and chest in the instep and ball of the foot, and those of the head in the toes. So, by shifting our weight back onto the heels and forwards onto the ball of the foot and the toes, we are stimulating all parts of the body in readiness for the day ahead.

In the third part of this dance we repeat the foot movements of the previous dance, **Step-by-Step,** but add coordinating arm movements. This forms an exhilarating crescendo of energy, which brings the PanEuRhythmy to a grand climax, leaving us energized physically, mentally and spiritually for all that the day may bring. There is a sense of picking up the themes of the previous dances and weaving them all together into a joyful grand finale. As the energy and emotion build up, it is like a stirring, profoundly joyful and triumphal Homecoming. Launching our day with PanEuRhythmy ensures a higher quality of day dawning.

This beautiful stately dance incorporates many of the features of previous PanEuRhythmy movements and also previews a movement from the next dance, **Sunbeams.**

26. Description of Movements for At Dawn: (96 bars in all)

There are **three** parts to this dance, each with its own set of movements. The music is played all the way through in each part, and in part 3 it is played through twice, making a total of 4 times in all.

The Bulgarian lyrics were written by **Peter Pamporov.** This last dance of the PanEuRhythmy is majestic and stately, in the tone of a triumphal finale. All face in a counter-clockwise direction throughout.

Part 1: (24 bars)

The music of each of the three groups of four bars is played twice, the first time while the right foot is leading and the second time as the left foot leads. Hands remain on hips.

Bar 1: <u>Diagram 26a</u>: Right leg swings around the left in a semi-circle and toes touch the ground on a diagonal in front of, and to the left of the left foot, then stretches out and swings back and around the left leg to a point on the same diagonal to the right of and behind the body.
Bar 2: Repeat the forward and back leg-swinging of bar 1.
Bar 3: Right foot steps forward followed by the left foot.
Bar 4: Right foot takes another step forward, then the left foot steps next to the right, so that the feet come together.

Bars 5-8: <u>Diagram 26b</u>: As the music of bars 1-4 is repeated, the above movements are repeated **inversely** – that is, with **opposite** feet.

The above eight-bar sequences of movements are repeated three times, until the music has been played through to the end. (24 bars)

Part 2: (24 bars) <u>Diagram 26c</u>:

The music of each of these groups of eight bars is again played through twice. Outer hands resting on our hips, we hold our partner's nearest hand up near our shoulders and take four very small steps forward, stopping with the left foot forward. We then swing arms with our partner down and back, then forward and up, twice in succession. As the arms swing back, our whole body **leans back onto our heels**, and as our arms swing forward, we **rise up on the balls of our feet**. Taking only very small steps enables the body to stay erect, tall and majestic.

Bar 1: Holding inner hands (Right palm down and Left palm up) between us at face or shoulder level, we take two small steps forward, first on the Right foot and then on the Left, the front parts of the feet

At Dawn

touching the ground first before stepping on the heels. At each step the
held hands give a gentle forward propulsion with a slight movement
of the wrists.
Bar 2: As in bar 1.

149

Bar 3: Left foot remains only slightly in front of Right. The whole body **leans back onto the heels,** as the inner held hands swing down and back, and the **toes of both feet are lifted up** from the ground. Then, as the arms swing forward and up, the body rocks **forward onto the balls of both feet** and the **heels rise up** gently from the ground.
Bar 4: As in bar 3.

The movements of these four bars are repeated until the music starts again from the beginning (24 bars.) The body is held tall, erect and majestic throughout.

Part 3: (48 bars)
The whole of the music is played through twice in part 3. Hands return to the hips, and the sequence of leg movements from the previous dance, **Step-by-Step,** are performed throughout part 3, with the addition of complementary arm movements horizontally out to shoulder level and back to the waist.

Bar 1: Hands on hips, Right foot steps forward, then Left foot.
Bar 2: Right foot steps forward, then the Left foot joins the Right foot.
Bar 3: <u>Diagram 26d:</u> Right leg extends itself to the RIGHT, toes just touching the ground, and both arms extend out SIDEWAYS to shoulder level, (palms down and fingers extended horizontally.) Right foot then steps back next to the Left foot again and hands return to the hips.
Bar 4: As in bar 3.

The music of Bars 1-4 is repeated as:
Bar 1: <u>Diagram 26e:</u> The Right leg extends FORWARD, toes just touching the ground, and arms extend horizontally FORWARDS at shoulder level. Right foot then steps back next to the left foot, and the hands return to the hips.
Bar 2: As in bar 1.
Bar 3: Right foot steps forward and the arms extend themselves FORWARDS, then the left foot steps forward and hands return to hips.
Bar 4: As in bar 3, except that Left foot comes to join Right, feet together.
Bars 5-8: The movements of the last 4 bars are repeated **inversely,** that is, with the LEFT foot leading throughout.

The simultaneous movements of the arms and legs are repeated to the end of the music. The RIGHT and LEFT feet lead in alternate groups of four bars, ending with the feet together. (48 bars)

27. Singing and Breathing

Here, finally, while standing still and facing each other in the circle, we break into song. As we come to the end of our "journey," we express to our friends and companions the joy we feel.

We open our hearts in love at the initial chord as we breathe in deeply, swinging our arms out from the heart forward in a horizontal arc round and back, ending with our arms straight out sideways from our shoulders, palms facing forward. Then, with the music we sing a full-throated "Ah"— that sound of fullness of awe and joyful wonder — our arms sweeping slowly forwards and round in a large, horizontal arc until our fingers touch our heart at the last note. This is repeated nine times, singing three times up the scale, three times down the scale, and finally the last three times, taking an extra deep breath and singing three notes up the scale, seven notes down and three notes up again.

This **Singing and Breathing** exercise, engaging our arms and voices, brings the energy built up in the PanEuRhythmy to a quieter and finer level of being, taking us inward into a subtler state of meditation. It enables us to open our hearts to one another and to the world, and to become more fully aware of the Joy and the Grace we share. It literally enables our hearts to sing.

27. Description of Movements for Singing and Breathing: (18 bars)

We all stand quietly around the circle facing the center. Usually the partners stand one behind the other, forming a double circle, but when the circle is small, people often prefer to stand in a single circle together.

As a long note is sounded on Lower G, the hands touch the heart, elbows out horizontally to the sides. We breathe in deeply and open our arms wide at shoulder level. Then, as a scale is played, we open our throats wide and sing "Ah!" up the scale of G major, all the time bringing our arms slowly forward and round till they touch the heart again. (This is repeated three times.)

A fourth long note is then sounded on Upper G, and we breathe in deeply, stretching our arms open wide, and then sing "Ah!" down the scale of G major, bringing our arms slowly round and horizontally back to the heart. (This is also repeated three times.)

Finally, as a seventh long note is sounded, this time on Upper D, we take in an extra deep breath. We then sing "Ah!" three notes up from B to D, a full scale down to lower D and up again to finish on middle G.
This is also repeated three times, after which we gently lower our arms to rest at our sides again.

28. Blessing

Finally, in the last movement, **Blessing**, we encompass all that vastness which we have experienced. We center it in our bodies, so that it stays with us, as we move into the day and out into the world.

We remain in our circle, facing the center with our arms loosely down by our sides. We then turn our palms to face outwards and slowly breathe in, as we raise our arms out, sideways and up until our fingers touch above our heads, signifying connecting with the oneness of Spirit. Slowly we then exhale and lower our hands to within a few inches from the top of our heads. Our hands then separate as we enter the world of duality (in the physical) and glide down, palms facing and close to our bodies, down the front of the two sides of our body until our arms once again hang loosely by our sides. We make this downward movement bringing the oneness of Spirit into the duality of our incarnate nature. As our hands rest by our sides, the energy continues to travel down through our fingers, down our legs, and meets under our feet, to contain our aura.

As we make this sweeping gesture, up and around our aura and then down our bodies, we say together the final Blessing:

> **"May the Peace of God**
> **and the pure Joy of God**
> **live in our hearts for ever!"**

The exact translation from the Bulgarian is:

> **"May Divine Peace abide,**
> **and may Divine Joy and Divine Gladness**
> **rise up in our hearts for ever!"**

Or we can simply say,

> **"May Love, Peace and Joy live in our hearts for ever!"**

28. Description of Movements for Blessing:

The musicians put down their instruments.

All stand facing the center, and together we all say the Blessing, as above.

We breathe in as we raise our arms slowly up over our heads, and breathe out as we lower our hands down the two sides of our body to rest by our sides — all in one slow, continuous movement.

Diagram 28a: Standing with our arms resting at our sides, we turn our palms forward and out, and then breathe in and say the first half of the Blessing as we slowly stretch our arms out sideways and up, till our fingers meet over our heads.

Diagram 28b: Fingers still touching, we bring our hands down to just above our heads or until we begin to feel our hair or our energy body.

Still saying the Blessing, our hands part slowly and caress our energy body down round our face, neck, upper chest and on down till our hands rest at our sides, fingers down.

This whole movement and the blessing are **repeated three times** in all.

Blessing

28a

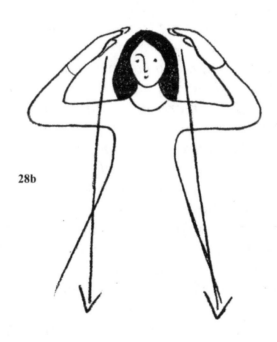

28b

The Teaching and Its Effect on My Life

Each dance of the PanEuRhythmy guides us gently
and lovingly opening us to the presence and power of Spirit
that is within us and in the Universe.
It is impossible to describe this experience accurately,
for it is beyond the realm of words –
but I know the very first time I heard the music
and the beautiful words that convey the meaning
of each dance, that I was **home.**
The dances are beautifully simple, yet their depth and power
is of a magnitude that cannot be measured.
As I dance I feel deeply enveloped in the essence
of Loving Spirit –I feel a union and communion
with that spiritual essence
that permeates all Nature and my being –
a spiritual exchange.
The PanEuRhythmy weaves threads of pure love –
PanEuRhythmy is LOVE IN MOTION – a moving meditation –
opening me to receive and give,
and healing whatever needs to be healed,
restoring me to balance and harmony.
As I go about my day I retain that feeling.
I feel more open and radiant –
as if I am walking on a cushion of flowing love.
I'm more open to my creativity,
and when I play the piano I feel an awareness of a deeper
dimension of my being and a stronger connection to the music.
The arm movements of the PanEuRhythmy
seem to be transported into my piano technique,
creating a natural fluidity and freedom.
I feel deeply nurtured by this beautiful dance.
Its teaching is complete and total – embracing all that life is.
PanEuRhythmy – a teaching – a truth – a gift –
an eternal guide weaving us through life –
its meaning ever deepening, ever expanding,
and from that still point within our hearts, we meet its gaze
and quietly say, "Thank you."
Beverly Weil, USA, 1993

Section 5

The Music and Lyrics

THE MUSIC

BEINSA DOUNO himself composed all the music,
as well as the words/lyrics for:
14. Missli !   15. Aoum
16. Izgreva Slunseto (The Sun is Rising)
27. Breathing and Singing
28. The final Blessing:
**"May Divine Peace abide,
and may Divine Joy and Divine Gladness
rise up in our hearts for ever!"**
"Hymn to our Earth Mother" (in the "Sunbeams")
We therefore usually sing the above songs in the original Bulgarian.

"Simply MIRACULOUS"

"I first learnt the PanEuRhythmy with Ardella in 1995.
From the first theoretical ideas
to the music and the movements,
I was touched by something beyond the normal.
The music was all-embracing, harmonious and transported me
to a high state of consciousness, I will say to the sublime.
Ardella asked for someone in the group
to assume responsibility for continuing to meet,
and I felt an inner voice saying, "You should do it."
Ever since, we have been practicing regularly in the park.
The PanEuRhythmy is simply MIRACULOUS.
Many doors have opened for me since I started this practice.
Passers-by are enchanted by the music and the dance.
Once a man quickly and quietly approached us,
saying he was amazed that the music had harmonized him
so much that he had to follow it.
Another time a blind woman sitting in a bench
by the end was crying with emotion.
She told us that we seemed like dancing angels!
How beautiful!
A man in a wheelchair would often sit in the center,
and received many benefits through the PanEuRhythmy.
A boy minding people's cars was enchanted
from the first time he heard the music. He asked for the music
to send to his mother in Bahia, far from Sao Paulo.
She said, "This comes from above; it is not a thing of the earth."
We have received many other similar responses
and always someone new comes and joins us every Saturday
when we gather to dance the PanEuRhythmy.
It remains for me to thank the great Master Beinsa Douno for
giving this wonder and to Ardella for having shared it with us."

— *Nadir Mercedes Tiveron, Sao Paulo, Brazil*
(Waldorf teacher and Paneurhythmy co-ordinator)

Vessela Nestorova

THE LYRICS
VESSELA NESTOROVA composed all the English lyrics,
and later modernized them together with BARNABY BROWN.
Vessela also composed the Bulgarian lyrics for the "Sunbeams."
OLGA SLAVCHEVA was inspired to write the Bulgarian words
for Movements 1-13 and 17-26.
PETER PAMPOROV composed the Bulgarian lyrics for the "Pentagram"

The Music & Lyrics
Introduction by Barnaby Brown

"Everyone should sing the PanEuRhythmy!"
   How many of us have become silent birds in a hostile wood where only an occasional nightingale sings out?
   Performing the PanEuRhythmy brings spring to the spirit, helping even the most reticent humans burst into song. If you have been deprived of the wholesome natural tonic of your own voice, then let the PanEuRhythmy restore it to you. Your song is sure to sound worse than some, better than others, though sure to write a smile on your heart.
"Joy is the natural state of life — PanEuRhythmy must be done joyfully."
"You are joining the angels — send out a wish for them to participate."
"To sing while dancing is to reap the richest benefit from the PanEuRhythmy."
   These are the words of Vessela Nestorova, who collaborated with Peter Deunov closely in the years 1941-1944, and wrote the Bulgarian lyrics for parts 1-6 of **"The Sunbeams"**, and her English lyrics for the whole **PanEuRhythmy** were written and revised in bursts of inspiration between 1940 and 1980. I shall never forget the experience of dancing in the Sofia forest in 1987. Under Communism, working people could not risk being seen joining in the PanEuRhythmy, so the circle was made up entirely of over-70s, perhaps 100 people. At least half of them sang from start to finish — an hour and a quarter of rapturous singing. What a way to start the day! Vessela told me:
   "Sing while you dance to engage the whole being. You must vibrate from head to toe and this is best done by singing, which has a great effect on every cell of your body. It also focuses your attention: nothing can disturb or distract you when you sing."
   "The consciousness must participate in every movement. Mind, heart, and will should develop simultaneously. Beautiful music ennobles the heart; rhythmic movement perfects our will; and singing enriches our mind."
   She had an evangelist's glow about her, a fervent love that spiritualized everything she did. It was a deep privilege to bring her some bread and basic provisions every week — the state pension was worthless in 1992 and she had no family to care for her. Her patience with me was remarkable; lesser souls would not have taken so kindly to

being edited by a 19-year-old. There were some awkwardnesses in her English lyrics, completed at Brother Kroum's behest in 1980. I wanted to iron these out with her collaboration, so that I could sing the PanEuRhythmy more comfortably myself, and to give her lyrics a higher chance of uptake throughout the English-speaking world. This involved explaining to Vessela the new sense of "gay", and numerous issues concerning word-stress or rhyme that didn't sit naturally for a native speaker.

Vessela soon became infected with enthusiasm, and the process of getting her approval for each solution was immensely instructive. I memorized her text and composed new lines on the tram to work, and each weekend we met in her tiny attic room to consider the revisions together. Her spiritual mentoring in these meetings set me up for life. Quoting from my notebooks:

"The PanEuRhythmy contains and promotes understanding of the entire teaching of the Master. It involves our every faculty, on which it also serves as a school making the greatest of demands, educating, ennobling, and spiritualizing all who partake .... Nothing is static or stiff — every cell in your body must vibrate in harmony with the movement. Be like water under the wind. Identify yourself with the melody and the rhythm. This is aided by singing."

"All things Divine come from within. Dance the PanEuRhythmy with your own movements, not the reflection of somebody else's. After versing yourself well in the written texts, dance as you feel from within, with all your soul. It is by giving expression to your soul and spirit that the whole effect becomes something more powerful."

It is important to bear in mind that every aspect of the creation of the PanEuRhythmy was collective. In 1940, Vessela set out to translate the Bulgarian lyrics by Olga Slavcheva, (published in 1935 while Vessela was studying in the USA). By 1980, however, Vessela's English lyrics had become a new composition in their own right, offering an enriching guide to the sense of the movements and illuminating the teachings of the Master. The manner in which Peter Deunov gave his disciples freedom to bring their own creativity to bear on the PanEuRhythmy inevitably gave rise to variants and differences of opinion. There are many who see variability as a bad thing, and we will never know the extent to which Peter Deunov was satisfied with the numerous, sometimes insistent suggestions which his disciples made.

Vessela was never dogmatic: the spirit behind each impulse was what mattered to her, not the physical form it took at any given date — and she abhorred religious adherence. This was precisely what Peter Deunov rose up against in the Bulgarian Orthodox church. The spirit of the Master's teaching, and the manner in which it unfolded paradise on earth, stayed alive in her, blossoming and growing, finding new forms appropriate for the time, place, and people she worked with.

"He gave the boards of wood and the wires; we had to make our own instrument. This is his teaching method; he is not prescriptive, just planting seeds."

Very few of the original lyrics were by Peter Deunov — only **"Thinking"**, **"Aoum"**, **"The Sun is Rising"**, and parts 7-10 of **"The Sunbeams"**. Even with the Master's words, Vessela reverently applied her own spiritual intelligence. Between 1941 and 1944, she collaborated with him on eight songs, helping him "to resuscitate, purify and transform folk music". Sometimes he provided the melody and asked her to compose lyrics (*Stavai dirshte* verses 2 & 3, *Pesen na dvete sestri*); sometimes he gave the lyrics and asked her for music (*Izvorche, Na rana prolet*); or he gave her germ ideas for both (*Pesen na jitenoto zurno*); or they collaborated on the text (*Tatuncho, Blagosloven kaza mamo, Ne li dumah*). Vessela was present when **"The Sunbeams"** was given. The Master originally sang *Tuk e rai,* "Here is paradise," but Vessela suggested to him *Tui e rai,* "This is paradise," and the Master was delighted. In a stream of inspiration, Vessela composed lyrics to parts 1-6 and came running back to him to see if they were acceptable. They were published in 1942 and are universally recognized as the poetic highpoint of the original PanEuRhythmy lyrics.

Throughout the dark years of Communist oppression, Vessela worked late into the night to spread the light of the Master's teaching abroad, translating lectures, composing oratorios, children's plays, songs, and poetry. In 1997, she approved these English lyrics as published in *Dance of the Soul*. Vessela passed away in 2004, and in this second edition, a few more revisions are introduced that I am sure she would have approved. They were requested by singers who memorized the 1997 edition, and Ardella and I are grateful to Harry Carr for assisting in this final polishing process.

Maria Zlateva playing violin in Rila

Acknowledgements

The following pages of music and lyrics could not have appeared without the wonderful hospitality poured on me while working in Bulgaria, the constant enthusiasm of my mother Alison, and the manifold assistance of PanEuRhythmy teachers the world over. Suggestions on how best to represent the music on paper have been gratefully received from numerous quarters; in particular, I thank Peter Ganev and Yoana Strateva for giving generously of their expertise. Above all, however, this work owes its existence to the fountain of wisdom, joy, and creativity that is Vessela Nestorova.

Barnaby Brown
Sofia, March 1997

Music for Healing

As a classical singer and holistic health practitioner
researching music for healing, I became interested
in Rudolf Steiner's work with art, music and Eurythmy.
Early one Spring morning in 1994,
I joined a group dancing on a hilltop,
but rather than Eurythmy,
it was Peter Deunov's Paneurhythmy...
It was immediately life-changing.
After dancing for an hour, and listening
to the blissful music that accompanies the dances,
I was surprised beyond surprise to see
that a discoloration and thickening that had persisted
on the whites of both eyes for months was completely gone.
In retrospect, I believe that the harmonious music,
physical exercise in a totally stress-free environment in nature
supported by beautiful spiritual energies,
activated and relieved a congested liver/gall bladder meridian.
I learned as much as possible that day
about the dance and the tradition,
and took tapes and instructions on the dances
with me when I returned to Virginia.
Although I have moved several times since then,
and seldom have a regular group with which to dance,
I have maintained over the course of nearly 15 years
some ongoing practice of my own.
I consider Paneurhythmy
and the vegetarian lifestyle which it promotes
to be an important part of my spiritual practice,
as well as an incredible gift of healing
and planetary transformation.
My home in a rural area accommodates five horses
who co-facilitate equine-assisted therapy services.
The horses always seem calmed and attentive
when the dances are ongoing:
I perceive them soaking up the vibrations
and envision incorporating Paneurhythmy into
therapeutic riding activities for enhanced results with clients."
Alicia Nation, Santa Fe, NM. January 2009

VIOLIN SCORE
A score for violin can be downloaded at
www.paneurhythmy.org/violinmusic.pdf
(This has fewer page turns than the vocal music, and is in the original octaves.)

THE PRONUNCIATION OF BULGARIAN

The transliterations provided below the Bulgarian lyrics are meant to be readable rather than scientific; the translations, word for word rather than elegant.

The following key should clarify any points of uncertainty.

VOWELS

Unlike the malleable sounds of English, Bulgarian vowels are crystal pure.

	Transliterated	Sung
у	oo/ou	(too)
о	o	(thought)
ъ	u	(fur)
а	a	(bard)
е	e	(bed)
и	i/ee	(see)

Be sure to distinguish *u* from *oo/ou*; also that *i* is not pronounced as in 'him', but always as in 'he'.

CONSONANTS

	Transliterated	Pronounced
ц	j	(decision)
ч	ch	(chip)
х	h	(loch)
в	v/f	a softer *v* than in English; often *f*
р	r	always rolled
с	s/ss	always soft

Be careful not to pronounce *s* as in 'rise', but always as in 'rice'.

165

Ardella Nathanael

I

1.-10. The First Day of Spring

Outward gestures synchronize with the right foot throughout.

1. Awakening, 9. Purification

1. Rise! A - wak - en! Spring is here.
9. On the __ breath of God we rise

O - pen your door to day - light clear.
through - all __ clouds and stor - my skies,

Full - ness of life for ev - ery - thing
pu - ri - fied if, come what may,

brings the __ first bright day of spring,
sow - ing __ beau - ty is our way,

brings the __ first bright day of spring.
sow - ing __ beau - ty is our way.

2. Reconciliation, 10. Flying

2. Na - ture is smi - ling, sun is __ shi - ning, hea - vens are blue,
10. Fly - ing, soar - ing, sun - shine __ pour - ing in and __ through

wa - ken - ing earth to life a - new.
ev - ery __ cell, we're born a - new.

---

* Any part of the melody may be sung an octave higher or lower so that it lies more comfortably in the voice.
 An edition for violinists and other instrumentalists is published separately.

3. Giving

Todor Papazov and Bojidar Simov leading the singing at Rila

"When I first heard the music of PanEuRhythmy,
my heart started beating more strongly.
I had the feeling that I had known it since long ago!
I felt incredible emotion and immense joy.
Tears were flowing from my eyes and I didn't know why.
I was sure of one thing only:
I wanted to dance PanEuRhythmy
and listen to this wonderful music.
Now, when I wake up, I play Peter Deunov's music
and start my day with PanEuRhythmy,
Thanks to this I am more joyful,
I smile at people and they smile back at me.
When difficulties come, I relax
and melt into the dance of the soul.
Then I perceive the world and its real values
in a different way,
and my problems disappear.
I find the solution or I meet people who help me."

Ewa Kapłan-Zielińska, Poland, May 2007
(Teacher of PanEuRhythmy on the Baltic)

11. Everà

12. Jumping

The hands spring apart immediately upon clapping to
resume their opening position: palms forward, arms upstretched.

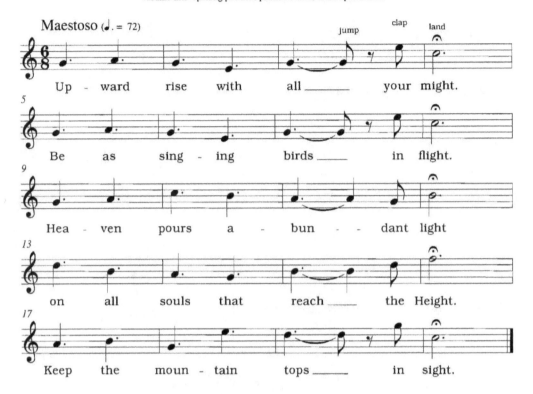

Maestoso (♩. = 72)

jump   clap   land

Up - ward   rise   with   all _____ your might.

Be   as   sing - ing   birds _____ in flight.

Hea - ven   pours   a - bun - dant light

on   all   souls   that   reach _____ the Height.

Keep   the   moun - tain   tops _____ in sight.

13. Weaving

The partner (initially) on the right takes two steps forward and remains in front throughout.
Only when weaving from left to right does the left foot begin, crossing over the right on the strong beat.

Moderato (♩ = 72)

Day   by day,   hour   by hour   weav - ing   on life's   loom ___

thoughts di - vine,   feel - ings fine   com - ing   in - to   bloom; ___

for   the new   Light and Love   now pre - pare we   am - ple room.

E - very day think and say that Light will come to - mor - row;

Love is now on its way to ba - nish fear and woe;

so we work and we pray for bright - er thoughts to know.

Weav-ing thus we take and give na-ture's gifts di - vine,___

learn - ing dai - ly how to live high - er lives sub - lime;___

weav-ing thus we all re - ceive the bles-sings of this time.

Day by day, hour by hour weav - ing on life's loom___

thoughts di - vine and feel-ings fine, for the new life mak-ing room,

for the life which turns the night to day and lights our up-ward way.

14. Think!

Begin up to the right. The slowly descending arc is gracefully paced.

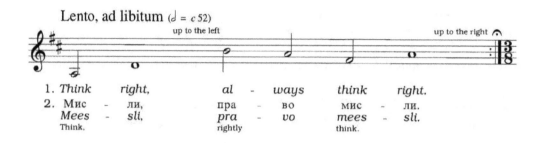

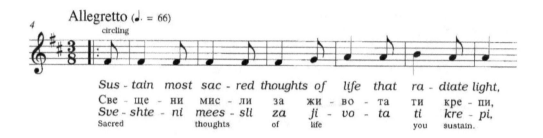

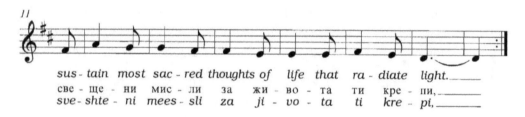

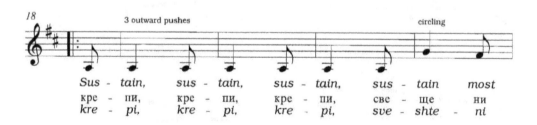

15. Aoum

Lento (♩ = 48)   (4 times)

А - ум,   А - ум,   А - ум, ___ Ом, ___ Ом, ___ Ау - мен.
A - oum,   A - oum,   A - oum, ___ Om, ___ Om, ___ Aou - men.

16. The Rising Sun

Adagio (♩ = 80)

1. Be - hold   the   ris - ing   sun,   send - ing   glo - rious   light,
2. Из - гря - ва   слън - це - то,   пра - ща   свет - ли - на,
   Iz - grya - va   slun - tse - to,   pra - shta   svet - li - na,
   Rising is   the sun,   it is sending   light.

fil - ling   life   with   joy   and   pure   de - light.
но - си   ра - дост   за   жи - во - та   тя.
nos - si   ra - dost   za   ji - vo - ta   tya.
bringing   joy   to   life   it is.

Moderato (♩ = 80)

6. then 7 cupping motions, bubbling up the sides of the body from thighs to ribcage

Liv - ing   pow- er,   spring-ing,   flow- ing   pow- er
Си - ла   жи - ва   из - вор - на   те - чу - ща,
Si - la   ji - va   iz - vor - na   te - choo - shta,
Power   living   springing   is flowing.

(2nd time) hands to chest

Liv - ing   pow- er,   spring-ing,   flow- ing   pow- er ___
си - ла   жи - ва   из - вор - на   те - чу - ща. ___
si - la   ji - va   iz - vor - na   te - choo - shta. ___

Give with the right foot. receive with the left.

Зун ме - зун, ___   зун ме - зун ___   би - ном ту ме - то. ___
Zoon me - zoon, ___   zoon me - zoon ___   bi - nom too me - to. ___
[no translation]

17. Square

Moderato (♩. = 60)

right out   together   left out   together

1. Bright is the morn, _____ filled with the frag - rance
2. Red is the east, _____ God's lov - ing lips its

sweet of flo - wers just born; white pearls of dew, a
bril - liant fore - head have kissed, fil - ling the mor - ning

gold - en crown her glo - rious head a - dorn. _____
air with vib - rant life and sac - red bliss. _____

clockwise

All na - ture sings! _____ All na - ture now with mu - sic

rings, _____ prais - ing the dawn, _____ prais - ing the

mor - ning new - ly born, _____ prais - ing the ris - ing

sun, the ra - diant fa - ther of the morn. _____

18. Beauty & 19. Flowing

18. Take 2 steps forward for every 1 back.

19. Take 4 steps forward for every 1 back. The left hand (upturned) receives the right every time.
fingers face to face and parallel. As the body turns, the hands glide apart and the left turns face downward.
The right hand then strokes the back of the left from wrist to fingertips as the arms spread out to 'fly'.

20. Overcoming

21. Joy of the Earth

Toes lifting, moving ever slightly forward

22.Friendship / Acquainting

As the arms spread out to 'fly' the fingertips momentarily touch, palms down.
After 'flying', whichever arm is forward swings back to join the other in an extended ellipse, raised to the rear:
in both cases the right hand turns face out to meet the left (which faces into the shoulder), fingers face to face and parallel.
With the next forward step, the hands glide apart as they pass below the chest,
leaving upturned left and downturned right ready to take your partner's hands.

Allegretto grazioso (♩. = 62)

swing apart   fly   ellipse to the rear   turn together   swing forwards   back   etc.

1. Touch of the hand   is   bles-sing a friend,   through
2. Кол - ко при - ят - но   пти - чен - це   пе - е
   Kol - ko pri - at - no   ptit -chen-tse   pe - e
   How   pleasantly   the little bird   sings

friend - ship and love   our   souls__ will   blend.__
и бла - го - дат - но   слън - це - то   грей.__
i bla - go - dat - no   slun - tse - to   grey.__
and what a blessing   the sun   shines!

Light- er our bur - den grows   when, with a friend so close,
Рос - ни ли - ва - ди - те,   све - жи по - ля - ни - те,
Ros - sni li - va - di - te,   sve - ji po - lya - ni - te,
Dewy   the meadows.   fresh   the grass.

feel-ings and thoughts so   high   meet eye to   eye.__
и - гра - ем ний и   пе - ем в ра - ни - на.__
i - gra - em ni i   pe - em f ra - ni - na.__
dance   we   and   sing   at early hour.

Bles-sings a - bun - dant flow   through ev - ery   soul,__
Жи - во - та е кра - сив   и и - зо - би - лен,
Ji - vo - ta e kras - sif   i i - zo - bee - len,
Life   is   beautiful   and   bounteous,

we feel the Hand Di - vine   mak-ing us   whole.__
че Бог над на - зи е__   ми - ло - стив.__
che Bog nad na - zi e__   mi - los - tif.__
for God over us   is   merciful.

23. A Beautiful Day

1st refrain: hands on hips.   *Verse 1:* hands rise alternately.   *2nd refrain:* inside hands hold constantly.
Verse 2 & last refrain: outside and inside hands hold alternately, the outer hands describing and retracing a spacious arc.

End - less_ beau-ty brings the_ spring: heav'n and_ earth with mu-sic_ ring,

liv - ing_ joy in ev - ery - thing, bran - ches,_ blos - soms,_

bub - bling__ springs. All a - round in daz - zling_ rings,

an - gels_ spread their rain - bow_ wings o - ver_ ev - ery_

(3rd time) Fine

soul that_ sings, o - ver_ ev - ery_ soul that_ sings.

1. As we_ wel - come each new_ day, from the_ sun a
2. Then God_ whis - pers in our_ heart, "Life Di - vine to -

shin - ing_ ray fills with_ fire our heart's de - sire to
- day you_ start. Praise with_ song the life you're_ giv - en,

see, to _ hear, to live a - new, learn - ing_ Love and
bless each_ soul up - on your_ path, e - ver_ grate - ful,

D.C.

Wis - dom_ true, learn - ing_ Love and Wis - dom_ true.
e - ver_ glad, e - ver_ grate - ful, e - ver_ glad".

24. How Happy We Are!

Repeat the entire song. If the extended version is played, join in again when the theme returns.

Allegro (♩. = 60)

3 steps forward for every 1 back, hands on hips

What de - light is liv - ing, giv - ing and re - ceiv - ing!

Live in a - do - ra - tion of the whole Cre - a - tion!

now 2 steps forward for every 1 back, with arm movements

Life is gift Di - vine, _____ beau - ti - ful, sub - lime; _____

liv - ing po - wers flow _____ mak - ing all things grow.

25. Step by Step

Allegretto (♩. = 64)

Step _ by step _ in life we rise, e - ver grow - ing good and wise;

ne - ver hur - ry, ne - ver stop, till _____ we reach _ the

high - est top. Fear - less and po - wer - ful, no - thing an ob - sta - cle,

con - scious - ly right - ing ev - ery wrong, step out stea - di - ly,

help _ out rea - di - ly, blaz - ing a path - way of light in song.

26. At Dawn

1. Right toe swings across and round behind steady left foot, hands on hips.
2. Four steps forward, with a little impulse from the held inner hands on each step.
3 & 4: four steps forward, hands stretching forward and returning to hips.

27. Breathing and Singing

28. The Blessing

<table>
<tr><td>either</td><td>or, stressing the accented syllables</td></tr>
</table>

May the peace of God
and the pure joy of God
rise and rest in our hearts
for ever.

(3 times)

Да пребъде Божият мир и да изгрее Божията радост
Da prebúde Bójiat mír i da izgré Bójiata rádost
May last forever God's   peace and may rise God's   joy

и Божието веселие в нашите сърца.
i Bójteto vessélie f náshte surtsá.
and God's gladness in our   hearts.

186

The Sunbeams

67

(last time) together, ready to return

share the joy of earth in her great new birth.

71

5. Some day earth will be _____ a pa - ra - dise of peo- ple free—,

75

with the an - gels in full har - mo - ny, spread - ing Love, _

79

build-ing God's Di - vine Cre - a - tion we, guid -ed from a - bove.

84

Left partners circle first. (When stationary, the right leg is lifted higher than the left.)

6. Flow - ing streams of bright beams bless us, un -
   In the round we are bound till God's Love

87

- bi - ased, from the sun. Keep - ing time with the rhyme
gen - tly turns the key. Eyes as high as the sky

91

we can now learn to live as one.
we're then drawn in - to har - mo - ny.

94

Share the joy of earth in her great new birth, _____
Love will let us free! Love is how to be. _____

98

share the joy of earth in her great new birth. (3 times)
Love will let us free! Love is how to be. (3 times)

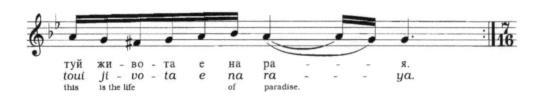

8. Рай, рай, рай, рай, ——— рай, рай, рай, —— рай, рай, рай, ———
   Rai, rai, rai, rai, ——— rai, rai, rai, —— rai, rai, rai, ———
   Paradise.

рай, рай, рай, ——— рай, рай, рай, ——— рай, туй е рай, ———
rai, rai, rai, ——— rai, rai, rai, ——— rai, toui e rai, ———
this is paradise.

рай, рай, рай, —— рай, рай, рай, —— рай, туй е рай, —— рай.
rai, rai, rai, —— rai, rai, rai, —— rai, toui e rai, —— rai.

9. Ка-жи ми, ка-жи ми, ка-жи ми слад-ки ду-ми две.
   Ka-ji mi, ka-ji mi, ka-ji mi slat-ki doo-mi dve.
   Tell me sweet words two.

Твой-те ду-ми две, слад-ки ду-ми две. ——— две.
Tvoi-te doo-mi dve, slat-ki doo-mi dve. ——— dve.
Your words two, sweet words two.

10. Туй е рай, туй е рай, туй е рай, туй е рай, рай.
    Toui e rai, toui e rai, toui e rai, toui e rai, rai.
    This is paradise.

The Pentagram

The music is repeated 5 times.

Moderato (♩ = 74)

1-2. *Here we come, beam - ing bright, ro - yal bear - ers of Light!*
3-5. Е - то веч и - дем ний, свет - ло-зар - ни лъ - чи;
E - to vetch i - dem ni, svet - lo-zar - ni lut-chi;
Here now come we, beaming rays;

From the heights we des-cend, help to earth here to lend.
цар - ски дар но - сим благ, ра - дост, мир и лю - бов,
tsar - ski dar nos - sim blag, ra - dost, mir i lyoo - bof,
a royal gift we bear. blessed: joy. peace and love.

Will you hear_____ our friend-ly call to - day?
свет - ли - на_____ и жи - ва кра - со - та,
svet - li - na_____ i ji - va kras - so - ta,
light and living beauty.

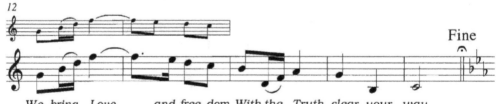

Fine

We bring_ Love ____ and free-dom. With the_ Truth clear your way.
сво - бо - да_____ за всич-ки - те ра - зум - ни ду - ши.
svo - bo - da_____ za fsich-ki - te ra - zoom - ni doo - shi.
freedom for all noetic souls.

17 The position of the Head remains constant: only the couple changes.

Truth and Jus-tice, Wis-dom, Love and Vir-tue are the paths Di-vine
Ний сме слън-че-ви лъ-чи на лю-бов-та, дош-ли в све-та,
Ni sme slun-che-vi lut-chi na lyoo-bof-ta, dosh-li f sve-ta,
We are sun beams of love, coming in light,

21

as the stars they shine, as the stars they shine!
зло да по-бе-дим, мир да въ-дво-рим.
zlo da po-be-dim, mir da vud-vo-rim.
evil that we vanquish. peace that we bring.

25 Which couple is now the Head?

Earth is re-born to-day, new life be-gins;
Със бла-гост, свет-ли-на, неж-на лю-бов
Sus bla-gost, svet-li-na, ne-ja lyoo-bof
With kindness, light and tender love

29

heav'n-ly an-thems, an-gel hymns to earth this new life brings.
нов жи-вот на ми-лост-та в све-та да въ-дво-рим.
nof ji-vot na mi-los-ta f sve-ta da vud-vo-rim.
a new life of compassion in light may we establish.

The Head and Left Hand turn to align themselves radially, then remain steadfast.
33 The Feet come into line with the Hands.

Fling high the ban-ners white, let mu-sic ring!
Със бла-гост, свет-ли-на, неж-на лю-бов
Sus bla-gost, svet-li-na, ne-ja lyoo-bof
With kindness, light and tender love

37 The Feet and Right Hand, pivoting on the Left Hand, arrive in line with the Head.

D.C.
ma
maestoso

Peace and friend-ship, joy un-end-ing brings the com-ing spring.
нов жи-вот на ми-лост-та в све-та да въ-дво-рим.
nof ji-vot na mi-los-ta f sve-ta da vud-vo-rim.
a new life of compassion in light may we establish.

193

THE LYRICS

The English Lyrics for the PanEuRhythmy, Sunbeams and Pentagram,
composed by Vessela Nestorova,
and updated in parts by Barnaby Brown, Harry Carr and Ardella Nathanael.

If a word or syllable is sung on two notes, it is followed by _.

Each section in italics must be repeated separately.

E D I T O R ' S   N O T E

This publication brings together the work and inspiration of many individuals, not least Vessela Nestorova. Her English lyrics were substantially written in 1941 and serve as a gateway to the Paneurhythmy for English speakers. A manageable portion of the Bulgarian text has been retained to prepare more dedicated Paneurhythmists for the task of learning the original lyrics, available in several editions. Movement cues have also been provided for convenient reference.

In Nos 14-16, No. 28 and sections 7-10 of 'The Sunbeams', the original text is by Petur Dunov. He set his students the task of writing lyrics to the remaining movements, a task that only Olga Slavcheva completed. Her text to Part I was published in 1935 and to Parts I and III in 1941; the text of Part II, completed by Vessela Nestorova, was published in 1942.

The lyrics constitute the third of three strands, namely the form, substance and sense of the Paneurhythmy. When understood, they feed the intellect, just as the movements tune the body and the music fires the spirit. No Paneurhythmy performance is complete without them.

Barnaby Brown, *Berlin, July 1997*

THE FIRST DAY OF SPRING

1. AWAKENING
Rise! Awaken! Spring is here.
Open your doors to daylight clear.
Fullness of life for everything
brings the first bright day of spring,
brings the first bright day of spring.

2. HARMONIZING
Nature is smiling, sun is shining, heavens are blue,
wakening earth to life anew.
Flowers, trees and birds and bees,
in colors bright and voices clear,
celebrate the spring that's here.

3. GIVING
Now be open to receive
all the blessings spring days leave,
beautiful gifts of life, thoughts bright and pure,
feelings sure, feelings of love that will endure,
thoughts_ as rays of sunshine in the spring,
gifts_ of gold this glad time now to us will bring.

4. ASCENDING
Then look up at yonder sun
and hail his work of wonder done.
Sing your praise unto the skies,
a joyful sparkle in your eyes.
Feel the sacred thrill!
With the birds the air with music fill!

5. ELEVATING
Higher, ever higher
everyone aspire!
Never think to stop
until you reach the most exalted mountain top!

6. OPENING

Cast off the clothes of the cold winter time,
bathe in the rays of today's sunshine.
Deeply breathe, absorbing all in sight,
Thanking God for the freedom and joy of light.
Shining above, the sun shows us the way,
filling our hearts with joy this springtime day.

7. LIBERATING

Finally, freed from chains of the past,
breaking away, liberated at last,
fly over lakes to mountain peaks snowy white;
there, at the doorstep of God, fold your wings and alight.
Blessed is the soul that, one with God, attains
life everlasting, life on higher planes.

8. CLAPPING

Joy like a spring from the heart let flow!
In everything is new life aglow.
Share the joy, the soaring of the soul;
Bless everyone on your way; give your love to all.
Singing the song of freedom, clap your hands,
sending rays of joy to farthest lands.

9. PURIFYING

On the breath of God we rise
through all clouds and stormy skies,
purified if, come what may,
sowing beauty is our way.
sowing beauty is our way.

10. FLYING

Flying, soaring, sunshine pouring in and through…
Every day we're born anew.
Flowers, trees and birds and bees,
in colors bright and voices clear,
celebrate the Spring that's here

11. EVERÁ

Dance in the dawn,
dance on the green and sparkling, decked with dewdrops lawn;
after a night of rest again in light be dressed.

[Breathe the morning air;]
Let the breezes waft away your care;
Rhythmic'ly dance with brooks and flowers fragrant, fair;
Graceful and free, step lightly on your way
On this inspiring bright spring day.

Dance in the dawn,
Welcome the rising sun the moment day is born;
Join in delighted song with Nature's dancing throng.

[Breathe the morning air;]
Let the breezes waft away your care;
Rhythmic'ly dance with brooks and flowers fragrant, fair;
Graceful and free, step lightly on your way
On this inspiring bright spring day.

12. JUMPING

Upward rise with all your might.
Be as singing birds in flight!
Heaven pours abundant light
On all souls that reach the Height.
Keep the mountain tops in sight!

13. WEAVING

Day by day, hour by hour, weaving on life's loom
Thoughts divine, feelings fine coming into bloom;
For the new Light and Love now prepare we ample room.

Every day think and say that Light will come tomorrow;
Love is now on its way to banish fear and woe;
So we work and we pray for brighter thoughts to know.

Weaving thus we take and give Nature's gifts divine,
Learning daily how to live higher lives sublime;
Weaving thus we all receive the blessings of this time.

Day by day, hour by hour weaving on life's loom
Thoughts divine and feelings fine, for the new life making room,
For the life which turns the night to day and lights our upward way.

14. THINK !
Think right, always think right.

Sustain most sacred thoughts of life that radiate light,
Sustain most sacred thoughts of life that radiate light.

Sustain, sustain, sustain,
sustain most sacred thoughts of life that radiate light.

15. AOUM
Aoum, Aoum, Aoum, Om, Om, Aoumen.

16. THE SUN IS RISING
Behold the rising sun, sending glorious light,
filling life with joy and pure delight.

Living power, springing, flowing power,
Living power, springing, flowing power.

Zoon meh-zoon, zoon meh-zoon,
Bih-nom toh-meh toh.

17. SQUARE

Bright is the morn,
filled with the fragrance sweet of flowers just born;
white pearls of dew, a golden crown her glorious head adorn.

All nature sings!
All nature now with music rings,
praising the dawn,
praising the morning newly born,
praising the rising sun, the radiant father of the morn.

Red is the east,
God's loving lips its brilliant forehead have kissed,
filling the morning air with vibrant life and sacred bliss.

All nature sings!
All nature now with music rings,
praising the dawn,
praising the morning newly born,
praising the rising sun, the radiant father of the morn.

18. BEAUTY

Graceful, beautiful and free,
Nature's music follow we.
High above an angel sings,
raising each hand a blessing brings.

Knowing only flowing motions soft as gold,
lovingly we let a bud of beauty unfold.

Like a lively brook in flow,
thus our hearts and minds will grow,
so we dance each day to be
graceful, beautiful and free.

19. FLOWING
Softly springing from the ground,
music ringing all around,
to the sky we lift our eyes,
spread our wings and, flying, rise.

Knowing only flowing motions soft as gold,
lovingly we let a bud of beauty unfold.

Like a lively brook in flow,
thus our hearts and minds will grow,
so we dance each day to be
graceful, beautiful and free.

20. OVERCOMING
"Nighttime is over!" says the sun;
Sadness and fear are overcome.
Steadily forward we bravely press,
through days of happiness, through distress.

Life is endless love and beauty,
and to do God's will our duty.

So press on, achieve your goal,
fill with light your hungry soul.
Heaven will help_ you on your way;
Love_ will cast_ all fear away.

Happy are they who see the track,
never a thought of turning back,
always of living for the Whole;
this_ is victory for the soul.

21. JOY OF THE EARTH
Build a new home where Joy can live,
build it of music angels give,
build it of Purity, build it of Light,
make it a palace large and white.

Let its windows open wide
welcome in the morning light:
Joy will come, that lovely queen;
readily she will enter in.
Now with music work begin.

Build with gladness,
build in the springtime morning;
as in heaven, sunlight your home adorning,
through every window pouring.

Slowly rising,
Heaven's hand in your labor,
ready to share with your neighbor,
this home of Joy Divine_,
beautif'ly flooded with sunshine,
shall be forever thine_.

22. ACQUAINTING
Touch of the hand is blessing a friend.
Through friendship and love our souls_ will blend.

Lighter our burden grows
when, with a friend so close,
feelings and thoughts so high
meet eye to eye.

Blessings abundant flow through every soul,
We feel the Hand Divine making us whole.

(This whole song is usually sung twice through.)

23. BEAUTIFUL DAY

Endless beauty brings the spring:
heav'n and earth with music ring,
living joy in everything,
branches, blossoms, bubbling springs.
All around in dazzling rings,
angels spread their rainbow wings
over every soul that sings.

As we welcome each new day,
from the sun a shining ray
fills with fire our heart's desire
to see, to hear, to live anew,
learning Love and Wisdom true.

Endless beauty brings the spring:
heav'n and earth with music ring,
living joy in everything,
branches, blossoms, bubbling springs.
All around in dazzling rings,
angels spread their rainbow wings
over every soul that sings.

Then God whispers in our heart,
"Life Divine today you start.
Praise with song the life you're given,
bless each soul upon your path,
ever grateful, ever glad.

Endless beauty brings the spring:
heav'n and earth with music ring,
living joy in everything,
branches, blossoms, bubbling springs.
All around in dazzling rings,
angels spread their rainbow wings
over every soul that sings.

24. HOW HAPPY WE ARE !

What delight is living,
giving and receiving!
Live in adoration
of the whole Creation!

Life is gift Divine,
beautiful, sublime;
living powers flow
making all things grow.

(Sing the whole song twice through.
If the extended version is played, join in again when the theme returns.)

25. STEP BY STEP

Step by step in life we rise,
ever growing good and wise;
Never hurry, never stop,
till we reach the highest top.

Fearless and powerful,
nothing an obstacle,
consciously righting every wrong,
step out steadily,
help out readily,
blazing a pathway of light in song.

Rising in life by slow degrees,
learning from Nature's flowers and trees
how in due season
deeply her reason
perfect completion sees.

Nature in winter is_ at rest,
like a good mother she knows_ best
when to awaken plants to life,
when birds should build their nest.

Ever glancing
for the dancing,
leaping sight of a deer;
ever listening
for the glistening
sound of running water clear.

Lost in wonder, breathe in the air!
Let the touch of God everywhere,
bringing to blossom all that is bare,
fill you with life,
fill you with love!
Gone is every care!

26. AT DAWN
Rise! New strength is born
with the first rays of dawn.

Loving every living soul,
sing and work to serve the Whole!
Glorifying God's great name
we achieve our highest aim.

All who love the light are free,
for their way they clearly see.

27. BREATHING AND SINGING
Ah-Ah-Ah-Ah-Ah-Ah-Ah-Ah!

28. THE BLESSING
May Divine Peace abide,
and may Divine Joy and Divine Gladness
rise up in our hearts for ever!

THE SUNBEAMS

1. Bright and glorious springtime dawn is breaking,
to new life the sleeping earth awaking;
with a light and rhythmic step we hail the rising day,
on the mountain meadows in array, with hearts full and gay.

2. Summits, lakes and fountains flowing
ring with music, sunshine, on the waters glowing,
life infusing, Nature ringing with our singing.
What a glorious spring! What a glorious spring!
Heaven opens wide its portals
blessings down to bring.

3. Draw from nature's boundless wealth
life abundant, glowing health;
give your gifts of Love to all people who are needy,
thus you will achieve your highest goal.

4. Step with grace,
turn your face
to the Source
whence all bounties flow.
Send your call
out to all
souls in need,
helping them to grow.
Share the joy of earth in her great new birth,
share the joy of earth in her great new birth.

5. Some day earth will be
a paradise of people free,
with the angels in full harmony,
spreading Love_,
building God's Divine Creation we,
guided from above.

6. Flowing streams
of bright beams
bless us, unbiased, from the sun.
Keeping time
with the rhyme
we can now learn to live as one.
Share the joy of earth in her great new birth!
Share the joy of earth in her great new birth!

(This whole verse is sung 3 times.)

7. In the round
we are bound
till God's Love gently turns the key.
Eyes as high
as the sky,
we are drawn into harmony.
Love will set us free!
Love is how to be.
Love will let us free!
Love is how to be.

(This whole verse is sung 3 times.)

ODE to our MOTHER EARTH (to be sung in Bulgarian.)
Ti si me, Mamo,
Tchovek krassif rodila,
Oomen da stana,
Dobre da misslia,
Dobre da liublia.
Tui zhivota e nah rah-ahyah!

Rai! (pronounced rah-ee, and repeated 27 times.)
Tooi eh rai! rai!

206

Kazhi mih! (3 times)
slatkih doomih dveh

Tvoyteh doomih dveh
slatkih doomeh dveh!

Tooi eh rai! (3 times)
Tooi eh rai! rai!

THE PENTAGRAM

(Words by Peter Pamporov)

Here we come, beaming bright,
Royal bearers of Light!
From the heights we descend,
help to earth here to lend.
Will you hear our friendly call today?
We bring Love and freedom. With the Truth clear your way.
Truth and Justice, Wisdom, Love and Virtue are the paths Divine;
As the stars they shine, as the stars they shine.
Earth is reborn today, new life begins;
heav'nly anthems, angel hymns to earth this new life brings.
Fling high the banners white, let music ring!
Peace and friendship, joy unending brings the coming spring.

Blessed with a vision that changed my life

As we moved in a circle, practicing "The First Day of Spring,"
I beheld a flock of orange angels — beings of light —
streaming down in front of the ancient trees surrounding us.
As we moved, I felt grace and peace such as I had never known.
I began practicing daily and enthusiastically inviting others.
Two years later, I joined the Rila Mountain camp in Bulgaria.
I was welcomed by Maria and Joro who had worked closely with
Krum Vazharov, the early disciple who hosted foreigners in Rila
during the time when this was absolutely forbidden.
Early the next morning, near the Lake of Purity,
as the mists swirled and the musicians sounded the first note,
hundreds of people stepped forward to dance as one.
The experience of unity, harmony, and oneness
transported me into another realm!
Then the work began in earnest.
That was the first of more than a dozen trips to Rila.
I began working with Maria, studying, helping to translate,
hearing stories of the early disciples, being of service..
I discovered that Paneurhythmy is the key
to a vast teaching and way of living.
Ardella, Maria and Joro gave me their blessing to teach —
after putting me through my paces in life as well as in the dance.
My precious connection with Ardella led me to Hawaii, England,
Australia, throughout the United States, and later to India,
as I committed to teaching the Paneurhythmy wherever invited.
Seeking to connect those who love the Paneurhythmy and spread
the word about Peter Deunov's many spiritual growth methods,
the not-for-profit, **Paneurhythmy: Circle of Joy** was created.
We also host a gathering in St. Louis at each summer solstice,
emanating the energy of peace and brotherhood
from the sacred ground by our Arch near the Mississippi River.
As I consider the importance of Paneurhythmy
in the evolution of the human soul, I am humbled.
Seeing the joy of those who join in, I am deeply grateful.
Knowing the transformations in my own life, I am beyond words.
May the seeds planted by all those who share this unique practice
germinate and flourish for generations to come!

Phyllis Thorpe, St Louis, MO, USA

208

Section 6

The Sunbeams

The Sunbeams

There is One who manifests as Love, as Wisdom, and as Truth.
There is One!
And all of Living Nature speaks of this One, this Great One.
Whenever Love, Wisdom and Truth are manifest,
Divine Spirit is present.
Peter Deunov (Beinsa Douno)

The Sunbeams are perhaps the most exquisitely lovely dances of all. Although they immediately follow the 28 movements of the PanEuRhythmy, they were not given until the early 1940's after the Pentagram. Peter Deunov felt that people were not yet ready to make the leap from the Physical level of the 28 PanEuRhythmy movements directly to the Divine/Spiritual level of the Pentagram, so he created the Sunbeams on the subtle/Spiritual level to create a bridge between the Physical and the Divine worlds of the other two dances. At that time he also expressed concern about the group's readiness for this dance, and even today, we may well feel hesitant about our readiness to participate, for it is a dance of the advanced beings of our planet connecting us with the central Source of Divine Love, Wisdom, and Truth. This dance calls for quiet focus on the inner meaning of the music and movements. When performed in an appropriate state of mind, the Sunbeams give rise to great joy, refreshment of spirit, calming of the nervous system and a heightened state of awareness.

In these dances, we are anticipating the coming era of harmony, peace, love, and light, and as we take part in these dances, we help to transmit and anchor this energy in the planet, as well as in ourselves and in the collective consciousness of Humanity. Seen in this light, we can understand that, in performing these dances early in the morning, we are rendering a Divine service. We are in this way serving both the world around us and ourselves, since the energies, as they pass through us, also transform and uplift our own consciousness.

Peter Deunov places great importance on meeting the sunrise:

"The Sun represents Divine Life which is constantly rising in the human soul. To renew yourself, rise early in the morning to receive the first ray of the Sun… and have a harmonious disposition in your soul, in order to receive the energies which the Sun abundantly sends us."

In the PanEuRhythmy, we trace the evolution of the human soul on this earth-plane through many stages and cycles of evolution. Now in the Sunbeams, we work at a level beyond the physical, where advanced beings, wholly dedicated to the outworking of the Divine Plan, are focusing their full attention on the Creative Source of all that is, and offering themselves as instruments, flutes through which the Divine music can be played and conveyed into all levels of Creation.

THE MUSIC of the SUNBEAMS is based on a traditional Bulgarian folksong, "Ratchenitsa," and has 7 beats in a bar — which for most non-Bulgarians takes some getting used to! It has a fast lively rhythm and is great fun to dance.

THE LYRICS TO THE SUNBEAMS, both in Bulgarian and in English, were written by Vessela Nestorova, who was very close to the Master and was expert in English. Her lyrics are particularly attuned to the deeper sense of the dance and are well worth singing. The "Ode to our Earth Mother" is always sung in Bulgarian, as well as the last few movements which are very simple and easy to sing.

THE SUNBEAMS AROUND THE SUN

We form a circle of twelve pairs, all facing the center which represents the Sun. Each pair is joined behind by up to five more pairs, thus creating a "Sunbeam." Each sunbeam therefore consists ideally of twelve dancers (six pairs in all, standing one behind the other.) The twelve sunbeams, (each composed of twelve dancers,) make a total of a hundred and forty-four dancers. When there are more than 144 dancers, as in the Rila Mountains in August, the others form a large circle around the twelve "rays" radiating out from the center, and do the same movements, facing and moving counter-clockwise throughout.

The twelve sunbeams radiating out from the center of the circle represent the twelve aspects, powers or manifestations of the Divine radiating out into Creation. The numbers twelve and twelve times twelve come up in many of the esoteric traditions of the world. The Bible talks of the twelve tribes of Israel, the twelve gates to the New Jerusalem, the hundred and forty-four thousand redeemed from the earth, the twelve powers of God. Astrology works with the twelve signs of the Zodiac, which are twelve gates through which the energy of the Universe is filtered into our lives. The day is divided into twice twelve hours, and even a musical octave consists of twelve semitones.

The first three parts of the Sunbeams consist of three different sequences, each first moving forward toward the center, then back and away from the center. In the three sets of movements toward the center we are aligning our consciousness with the Divine Source: through the Head, the Heart, and the Will respectively. These sequences correspond with the ancient Vedic teachings of India, which teach that there are three main paths to the Divine: Jnana Yoga (the path of the Head), Bhakti Yoga (the path of the Heart), and Karma Yoga (the path of Willing service.) The movements away from the center represent our carrying the energies we have just received and passing them on toward the outer circle, in other words, out into the world. Throughout this dance we face the center, symbolizing our focus on the Divine Source.

1. CONNECTING WITH THE DIVINE THROUGH THE MIND
The first sequence is an expression of connecting through the Head with Divine Mind. The movements are bright and energetic, and the hands move forward and up in comparatively straight lines, expressing the electric quality of mental energy. The two arms swing forward and up, finishing with a light clap as we step forward onto the right foot. When we step onto the left foot, the two hands swing forward and reach reverently forward and up. This sequence is repeated until the third clap, after which our hands go onto our hips, (and remain there until we sing the **Ode to our Earth Mother.**)

We then start the movements back and lovingly take the energy we have received out into the outer circle of the world. The three sequences of movements back are all the same. At each step we swing the front leg in a semi-circle round to the back, with a little bounce on the supporting leg. These circular movements symbolize the energy of the heart, and remind us how vital it is that Love always be the guiding force in our expression of Divine energy out in the world.

2. CONNECTING WITH THE DIVINE THROUGH THE HEART

The second sequence of movements towards the center connects us through the Heart with Divine Love. The gentler circling movements and softening of the legs express the warm magnetic quality of heart energy, contrasting with the straighter, sharper movements of the first sequence. We swing one leg twice forward and back in an arc around the other leg, and then step forward, after which we repeat the sequence in reverse with the other leg.

3. CONNECTING WITH THE DIVINE THROUGH THE WILL

This third sequence symbolizes the deliberate forward movement of the Will, expressing itself in action under the guidance of the Head and the Heart. Here, while bouncing on the supporting leg, we first raise the right knee and gently tap the ground with our toes twice, and then step forward. The sequence is then repeated with the other leg. The tapping indicates that action has to be expressed on the earth in physical ways. The bending of the supporting knee shows that we have to be flexible and willing to bend as we offer service in the world.

These three sequences, connecting ourselves with the Divine in the three different forward movements, and their counterparts, carrying the blessings out into the world in the backward movements, complete the first, essential stage of the work of the Sunbeams. In order to be fully aligned with the Divine Plan, we want to start our work by infusing ourselves totally with the energy of the Divine. There is a striking correspondence here in these three sequences with that universal prayer which unites us all — **the Great Invocation**:

"From the point of Light within the Mind of God
Let Light stream forth into the minds of men.
Let Light descend on Earth.

From the point of Love within the Heart of God
Let Love stream forth into the hearts of men.
May Christ return to Earth.

From the center where the Will of God is known
Let Purpose guide the little wills of men,
The Purpose which the Masters know and serve.

From the center which we call the race of men
Let the Plan of Love and Light work out
And may it seal the door where evil dwells.

Let Light and Love and Power restore the Plan on Earth."

4. CIRCLING OUR PARTNERS

The next sequence concerns itself more specifically with our work on the human plane. In human life and relationships we express the Divine Plan by serving one another in a spirit of Love, and this is expressed in the dance by each partner circling the other. The partner being circled continues the previous movement of gently bouncing and tapping the ground with the toes, expressing, in so doing, their ongoing commitment to Willing Service of the Divine. And in between each circling, together the partners do more of the bouncing and tapping steps, expressing their common desire to align with the Divine Will and Purpose, as they move together in rhythm with the Divine music.

After both partners have completed the circling sequence, both partners once more simultaneously circle each other in opposite directions, and again finish with the tapping steps performed in rhythm together. The simultaneous circling has the effect of the two circles intersecting one another, forming a "vesica pisces" which, in the early Christian tradition, symbolized the womb in which the Christ Child can evolve.

The Path of Willing Service, therefore, is also an integral part of this fourth sequence, where we focus on the expression of Divine Service in everyday living, as Mother Teresa so powerfully exemplified for us. In a spiritual partnership, it is important that the one being served is himself anchored in Willing Service to the Divine, so that Service to one's partner can also become Service to the Divine.

In ordinary human living it is easy for this circling to become limiting both to oneself and to one's partner, but the original Divine intention in creating human beings male and female was that we would comfort and support one another in our Divine destinies on this earth plane. In the original Vedic ideal of marriage, both the husband and the wife were encouraged to see the Divine in one another, and the marriage ceremony incorporates a joint circling of the Divine Fire. In her book, *The Spirit of Intimacy,* Sobonfu Some portrays this as also being the guiding ideal in the concept of marriage and community among the West African Dagara people. This mutual service of the Divine in one another elevates all forms of spiritual partnership including marriage to a level beyond the normal entanglements of human relationship, and leads us to the next sequence, which is a beautiful sung eulogy of the miracle produced by the "marriage" of Father Spirit and Mother Earth.

5. ODE TO OUR EARTH MOTHER

This is one of the most beautiful parts of the whole PanEuRhythmy. The Christchild in each dancer, now fully born on the human plane, sings a song of praise to our Beloved Mother Earth who has enabled the manifestation of Eternal Spirit on the level of Physical Matter — a miracle beyond human conceiving.

As we all sing this **Ode** together, we stand still, facing the center holding our partner by both hands. Our inner hands are raised up beyond the shoulders, while our outer arms form a gentle curve a little lower than the solar plexus across our forward-facing bodies, representing our loving, harmonious linking together while our attention is jointly and fully turned toward the Source. The heavenward sweep of our inner arms represents the rising of our heart energy in prayer and adoration and thankfulness, which opens our conjoined hearts to receive Divine gifts and Inspiration.

This song which we sing together is an exquisite soulful expression of love and gratitude to our Earth Mother for creating us so beautifully, with the capacity to fully evolve our faculties of intuition, thinking and feeling, which can lead us respectively to the full expression of Wisdom, Truth, and Love. It is this evolution of consciousness which eventually makes possible the full manifestation of Paradise — the Plan on Earth.

6. CLAPPING

The joy released by this incredible feat of incarnating and expressing the Divine on the level of Matter finds rapturous expression in clapping and gently moving to the lively rhythm of the music. The right hand claps, palm down, and then bounces back up and over to the right in an arc, finishing with the palm up. The left hand performs a smaller arc, as it claps, palm up, moving towards and away from the right hand.

Energy moves through the body out through the right arm and hand and in through the left. This teaching of the Master Peter Deunov is also in line with Chinese medicine where acupuncture meridian charts depict how energy moves out through the right arm and hand and in through the left. So in the previous movement, when holding the partners' hand, the left palm expresses receptivity and is always up, while the right palm faces down, expressing directing of energy.

7. INVOKING THE DIVINE

The next movement is a poignant and soulful calling upon the Divine to speak the words of Love that every human Soul longs to hear. The dancers stand in place cupping their hands together like a rosebud in front of the heart, the wrists held close to one another and the fingers up like the petals of a flower. As they sing the words, "Kaji mi" ("Give me" in Bulgarian), they open the fingers and palms away from each other, symbolizing the opening of the rose of the heart in the sunshine of Divine Love. The final words, "tvoite dumi dve, sladki dumi dve" ("your two words are words of sweetness"), express the soul's steadfast faith that the will of God is always loving. (In Bulgarian, the expression, "I love you" consists of two words only!)

8. THIS IS PARADISE!

The final movement of the Sunbeams is ecstatic. It expresses not only the faith, but also the experience, of the Divine Will, when fully manifest on the Earth plane, creating nothing less than Paradise. Still facing the center the partners move slightly apart, their arms undulating out from the shoulders sideways, as if flying, while they sing over and over again **"Tui e rai! Tui e rai!"** ("This is Paradise!") and express the Joy of creating Heaven on Earth.

Dancing Sunbeams near St Louis

Description of Movements for the Sunbeams:

THE SUNBEAMS AROUND THE SUN consist of 12 pairs (24 dancers) standing in a circle, all facing the center, and behind each pair are 5 more pairs, (making a total of 144 dancers.) Each individual sunbeam radiating out from the center therefore consists of 6 pairs (12 dancers in each sunbeam.)

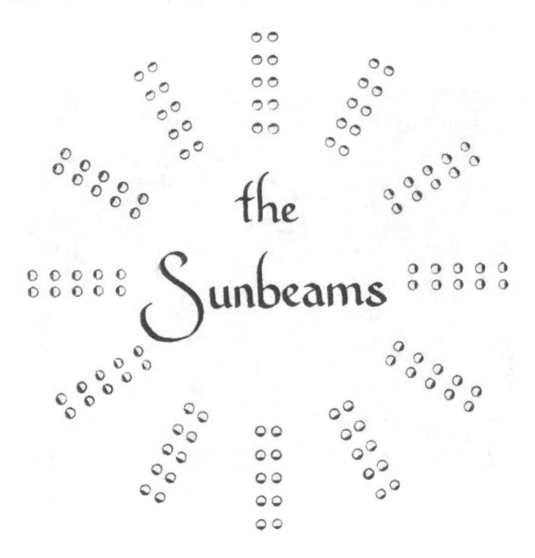

There needs to be about one meter's distance between the dancers in each sunbeam. It is best to have the shorter people in front, (or, in any case, those who know the movements well,) so that those behind can see and coordinate with those in front.

The first 3 parts are each in 2 parts:
Parts 1A, 2A and 3A moving FORWARDS towards the center, and
Parts 1B, 2B and 3B moving BACKWARDS away from the center.
It is good to sing throughout, but in any case the "Ode to our Earth Mother" in Part 5 needs to be sung.

1A: CONNECTING WITH THE CREATOR THROUGH THE MIND (15 bars) **Count 15 movements forward.**

This first sequence consists of a swinging of the two arms from the right side of the body forward to the left and up, finishing with a step forward with the right foot and a clap. Then, as we rock back on the left foot, the arms swing back down to the left, after which, as we are stepping forward with the left foot, they swing forward and up to the right until both hands are stretching forward and up to the right, palms down.

Starting Position: <u>Diagram 1a</u>: All stand facing the center, weight of the body back on the Right leg, Left leg slightly in front, both hands back to the Right of the body, palms down.

Bar 1: <u>Diagram 1b,1c</u>: Stepping forward onto the Left foot, the hands swing gracefully forward and up.

Bar 2: As the Right foot steps forward and the Left heel lifts, the hands continue on up and clap lightly to the Left.

Bar 3: Swinging the arms back and down to the Left, the body rocks back onto the Left foot, the Right leg bends and lifts off the ground, with the toes pointing down.

Bar 4: Stepping forward onto the Right foot, the arms swing forward and up, as in bar 1.

Bar 5: <u>Diagram 1d, 1e, 1f</u>: Stepping forward onto the Left foot, the Right heel lifts, the arms stretch out and the hands reach reverently forward and up and slightly to the Right, palms facing down.

Bar 6: Swinging arms back and down to the Right, body rocks back onto Right foot, Left leg bends and lifts off the ground, toes pointing down.

This sequence is repeated until the third clap (see bar 2), after which our hands immediately go to our hips, as we rock back onto the Left foot, Right foot remaining forward, (as in bar 3.)

Sunbeams 1 and 2

1a

1b, 1c

1d, 1e, 1f

1g

2a

2x

2b

1B: RETURNING: (Same 15 bars repeated) **<u>Diagram 1g</u>:**
Count 15 movements back.
Hands on our hips, thumbs to the back. Starting with the Right foot, in each bar the front foot swings back in a semi-circle around the other and steps (on the beat) to the back of the other, the supporting leg bouncing as we do so. On the 15th step the weight of the body stays on the Left leg. The heels barely touch the ground throughout, bringing a light, springing, dancing quality to the movements.

2A: CONNECTING WITH THE CREATOR THROUGH THE HEART: (16 bars repeated =32 bars in all) **<u>Diagram 2a</u>:**
Count 20 movements forward.
In this second sequence the hands remain on the hips throughout, as we move forward again towards the center, this time with a circling movement of the feet.
We swing one leg forward and back twice in an arc around the supporting leg which bounces each time we swing, and then we take a step forward. The sequence is then repeated with the other leg.
For balance and stability, as well as to feel the full energy of the movement, it is helpful to focus on a point in the mid-lower back and feel the moving leg swinging freely from the hip rather than from the knee.

Bar 16: Right leg swings forward around the Left, and toes delicately touch the ground in front and slightly to the Left of the Left foot.

Bar 17: Right leg swings back in the same semi-circle around the Left to gently touch the ground at the back and to the Right of the Left foot.

Bar 18: As in Bar 16.
Bar 19: As in bar 17.
Bar 20: Right foot steps forward and takes the weight of the body.

Bars 21-25: Left foot now takes over and repeats the same movements as in the last five bars.

This 5-bar sequence is repeated 6 times (30 bars) and in the last 2 bars (before **Returning**) the Right foot circles the Left once more forward and back, as in bars 16 and 17, (before stepping backwards in the first bar of the next **Returning** sequence.)

2B: RETURNING: (20 bars) **<u>Diagram 2b</u>:**
20 circling and bouncing steps back (as in Part 1B), ending on left foot.

Sunbeams 3,4,5

3

3x

4a

4b

3x

3x

5

3A: CONNECTING WITH THE CREATOR THROUGH THE WILL:

(18 bars repeated= 36 bars in all.) **Diagram 3:**

Count 12 movements forward.   Hands remain on the hips. First we raise the Right knee and spring down and up on the Left leg in order to gently tap the ground twice with the toes of our Right foot and then step forward.

We then repeat the sequence with the opposite legs.

Bar 53: Right knee raised, the Left supporting leg bends on the first beat of the bar then immediately springs up again, enabling the Right toes to gently tap the ground.

Bar 54: As in bar 53.

Bar 55: Stepping forward onto the Right foot, the Left leg springs up and forward.

Bar 56: Left leg remains bent and off the ground, as the Right leg bounces down and up and the Left foot taps the ground with its toes.

Bar 57: As in bar 56.

Bar 58: Left foot steps forward and the Right springs up and forward.

This sequence (of the last six bars) is repeated six times, ending with the body on the Left foot.

3B: RETURNING: (13 bars) Count 12 movements back.

12 circling steps backwards (as in Part 1B,) ending on the left foot.

4. CIRCLING OUR PARTNERS: Diagram 4a:

(10 bars then 8 bars, then the 18-bar sequence is repeated.)

Count 18 movements, and repeat.

This sequence is in 6 parts (A-F) which are repeated.

The partners start side by side, hands on their hips, weight on the Left foot.

As we walk, we let the toes touch the ground before the heels.

A: (10 bars)The partner on the Left takes ten lightly springing steps clockwise around the Right partner. **The partner on the Right** remains in place, dipping lightly down and up on the supporting Left leg in each of 4 bars, the Right knee raised with the lower leg relaxed and toes gently tapping the ground at each dip.

In the 5th bar the Right foot steps back down next to the Left foot, then in the 6th bar the Left knee is raised and the movements are repeated, this time with the Right leg supporting and bending.

223

B: (8 bars) <u>Diagram 4b</u>: Both partners side by side dip down and up in each bar, 3 times on the Left leg, with the Right knee raised, and in the 4th bar the feet are together again.
The 4 movements are repeated on the Right leg with the Left knee raised.

C: (10 bars) The Right-hand partner takes 10 steps counter-clockwise around the Left partner. **The Left-hand partner** raises the Right knee and dips down and up on the Left leg in each of 4 bars, bringing the feet back together in the 5th bar, then repeating the movements on the other leg (as in A above.)

D: (8 bars) As in B, **both partners** side by side dip down and up in each bar, 3 times with the Right knee raised, then the feet return together in the 4th bar.
The 4 movements are then repeated with the Left knee raised.

E: (10 bars) Both partners circle one another simultaneously in opposite directions in two intersecting circles. The partners connect with the eyes as they pass one another, first to their Left, then to their Right.

F: (8 bars) As in B.

The whole sequence (A-F) is then repeated from the beginning.

5. ODE TO OUR EARTH MOTHER: (14 bars repeated) **<u>Diagram 5</u>:**

Ti si meh, Mamo,
Tchovek krassif rodila,
Oomen dah stana,
Dobreh dah Misslia,
Dobreh dah Liublia :
Tui zhivotah eh nah Rah-ahya !

As the couples sing this **Ode**, they stand in place, all looking towards the center of the circle and holding each other by both hands. Their inner arms are raised above shoulder level, with their outer arms a little lower than the solar plexus forming a gentle curve across their forward-facing bodies, representing their loving, harmonious linking together while their attention is fully turned toward the Source. The heavenward sweep of their inner arms represents the rising of their heart energy in prayer and adoration.
The whole Ode is sung through twice, sometimes three times.

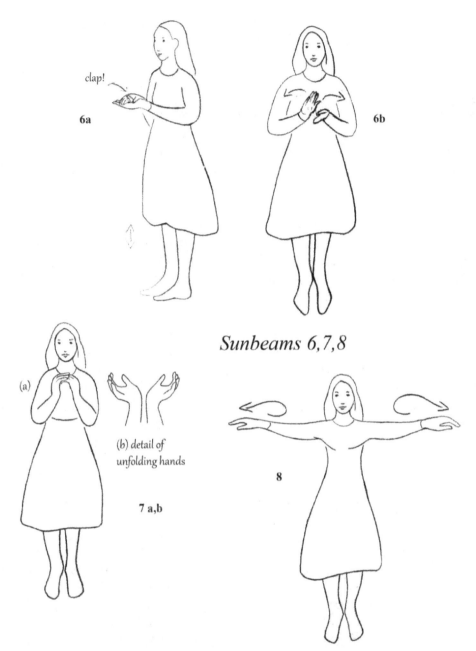

clap!

6a

6b

Sunbeams 6,7,8

(a)

(b) *detail of unfolding hands*

7 a,b

8

6. CLAPPING: (13 bars repeated: 26 claps) <u>**Diagrams 6a and 6b:**</u>
Singing **Rai, rai, (**Paradise,) we clap at the level of the heart on the first beat of each of 26 bars, the whole body gently moving to the lively rhythm of the music and swaying in expressions of rapturous joy.
The right hand claps, palm down, and then bounces back up and over to the right in an arc, finishing with the palm up. The left hand performs a smaller arc, as it claps, palm up, moving towards and away from the right hand.

7. INVOKING THE DIVINE: (5 bars repeated, then 4 bars repeated)
Kaji mi, kaji mi, kaji mi slatki doumi dve!
(Give me, give me two sweet words of love!)

Diagram 7a,b: We stand in place cupping our hands together like a rosebud in front of the heart, wrists held close to one another and fingers opening up like the petals of a flower. These gestures symbolize the opening of the rose of the heart in the sunshine of Divine Love.
(First the Right hand is folded over the Left, then the Left hand over the Right, and so on, alternating to the end.)

A: 5 bars: We sing the words, **Kaji mi,** in each of the first 3 bars, bringing the fingers and palms together (on **kaji**) and opening them away from each other (on **mi.**) In the 4th bar we bring them together on **slatki doumi** and open them again on **dve** in the last bar.
  This whole sequence is then repeated.

B: 4 bars: As we sing **tvoyti doumi dve** (your two words...) in the first 2 bars the Left hand remains over the Right, and then in the last 2 bars, as we sing **slatki doumi dve** (...are words of sweetness,) the hands open out and we look up in a glance of loving thankfulness. These final words, **tvoyte dumi dve, sladki dumi dve,** are then repeated, the Right palm covering the left this time and then both palms opening.
These last words express the soul's steadfast faith that the will of God is always loving.

8. THIS IS PARADISE! "Toui e Rai!" (5 bars repeated)
Diagram 8:
Still facing the center the partners step slightly apart, their arms undulating out from the shoulders sideways, as in **Flying**, while singing "Toui e rai!" (This is Paradise!) in each bar and "rai" in the last. The movement is lighter and more evocative of flying if the arms undulate up on the first beat of each bar, then float down in the latter half of each bar. The final movement of the Sunbeams is ecstatic. It expresses our feelings of blissful Joy at creating Heaven on Earth.

An unlikely journey
from secular materialism toward spirituality
began nearly 20 years ago
when I was introduced to the Paneurhythmy,
brought within a few miles of where I live
by uniquely intrepid, devoted, globe-trotting Ardella Nathanael.
A new acquaintance had put the music quite literally
in front of me —in a cassette player on my coffee table;
even in that form it called to the soul I didn't know I was.
As if against my will, I was drawn to it.
Soon, inspired by Ardella's brilliant teaching,
with will engaged and intent on making it my own,
I set out with determination to learn every movement by heart.
In this process, it is an understatement to say that
I have met wonderful people and traveled to special places.
Although not always easy,
all the experiences — inner and outer — are treasures.
The Paneurhythmy, which I am now blessed to share with others,
is a source of unfailing sweetness and goodness,
nourishing my slow-growing faith in the best possible way.
For this gentle, potent schooling for the human being,
I am unendingly grateful.

Elizabeth Weiss, California, USA — 2012

SECTION 7

THE PENTAGRAM

Peter Deunov's original diagram in Cyrillic script depicting the spiritual evolution of the Soul, first around the outer circle, then along the path of the pentagram itself, and finally culminating in the center.

The Pentagram (a five-pointed star) is a sacred symbol which has been used since ancient times by Pythagoras and others as a spiritual symbol and as an anchor for spiritual teachings. Quite early on in his teaching Peter Deunov introduced the idea of the Pentagram as a symbol for spiritual evolution, and gradually the inner meaning was revealed to him in a much more profound way than (as far as we know) to any other spiritual teacher.

THE SYMBOLISM OF THE PENTAGRAM

"In the Fulfilment of the Will of God lies the power of the human Soul."

These words surround the Pentagram, and, as we study it, they gradually take on new depths of meaning. The outer circle represents the ordinary way of development for humanity, while the inner path of the Pentagram depicts the path of true Discipleship.

The Pentagram, a five-pointed star, symbolizes the cosmic human being, Cosmic Man. The five points represent the five directions in which a human being needs to grow, in order to become self-realized. The upper point arises from the head, Truth, and the color for Truth is blue. The left-hand point arises from the heart and directs us towards Love, and the color for Love is pink. The right-hand point arises from thinking (which, according to Peter Deunov, is associated with the right side of the body and the left brain,) and directs us towards Wisdom. The color for Wisdom is yellow, the color of sunshine, brilliance, light, seeing everything clearly. These three sublime qualities — Love, Wisdom, and Truth — are qualities of Spirit.

In incarnated human beings, these spiritual qualities have to manifest on the earth plane in a practical way, so, below the Left Arm of Love is the Left Leg of Virtue or Goodness (the human manifestation of Love in everyday living), and below the Right Arm of Wisdom is the Right Leg of Justice (the practical outworking of Wisdom in human life.)

Goodness and Justice, therefore, form the two "legs" which support the qualities of Spirit in the human world. The color for Goodness, the Left Leg, is green, the color that growing plants produce under the action of the Sun, as the heart expresses itself in Goodness under the action of Divine Love and Light. The color associated with Justice, the Right Leg, is orange, which is a combination of the yellow of Divine Wisdom and the red blood energy of the flesh and the earth.

A good symbol for the fully self-realized human being is the diagram by Leonardo da Vinci of a man standing within a circle. The man standing within a square represents the human state of sleeping consciousness and imprisonment in matter. As he awakens and extends himself to his full potential, he finds himself evolving into the dimension of Spirit, represented by the circle, and his body enters the shape of the pentagram. His arms are no longer merely instruments to connect with, and act within, the earth plane. They are becoming like wings to carry him Heavenward. They are developing the ability to act under the direction of Love and Wisdom, raising the head to connect with Truth. The legs also are no longer static. They are open now and move within the circle of Spirit.

Although Peter Deunov only outlined the meaning of the Pentagram, as with Jesus' parables, we discover more and more meaning as we study them ever more closely. Personally, I find that nothing is accidental in the diagram. For instance, although the journey on the outer circle is outside the Pentagram itself, it seems to me that the influence of the great rays of Justice and Virtue, Love, Truth and Wisdom, is felt as one moves past their respective domains.

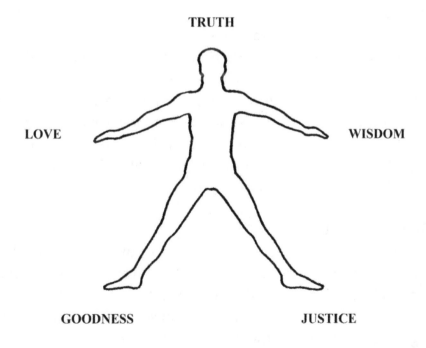

TRUTH

LOVE

WISDOM

GOODNESS

JUSTICE

THE SYMBOLS ON THE OUTER PATH OF NORMAL EVOLUTION

THE SWORD

The words around the circle, "In the fulfillment of the Will of God lies the Power of the human Soul" start at the bottom, and so does man's evolution — between the rays of Justice and Goodness — with the picture of the sword, which depicts violence. Even people who are not very evolved have a concept of good and bad, fair and unfair, just and unjust. People have fought and quarreled and argued over these concepts all through the ages, and this violence produces suffering. People can go through a few years or many lifetimes working with these concepts, until finally suffering itself acts as a purifier and distills the essence of our being. Our hearts become softened and our nervous systems more highly attuned. Under the power of all these experiences we begin to wake up. We move away from violence and begin to develop Goodness and to understand Justice.

THE CUP

The cup lies between the rays of Goodness and Love. As we seek to lead a life of Goodness, our hearts begin to open to others and to learn Love. A cup is a very different shape from a sword. A sword is straight, pointed, and aggressive, the point representing "my" will, with scant consideration for yours. A cup is rounded and inclusive; a cup nurtures, holds and contains. We learn not only to drink from the cup of suffering, but also to distill from it the ability to love and share goodness. We open to the power of Love.

THE BOOK OF LIFE

The Book of Life lies between the rays of Love and Truth. Having come under the influence of Love, we now want to understand and learn and know, so we study the Book of Life. Gradually we begin to understand the laws of Nature and work consciously with them. We are learning discernment and being drawn towards Truth.

THE CANDLE

The candle lies between the great rays of Truth and Wisdom. As we apply the Truth that we know, a "candle" is lit within us, and we learn to see truly. We learn to live more consciously, we apply what we know, and so develop discernment, and our well-being increases. More and more we find we are no longer victims, but, as we learn Wisdom, we can take charge of our lives and be more profoundly useful in the world, and so find greater fulfillment and happiness.

THE SCEPTRE

The scepter lies between the rays of Wisdom and Justice, and symbolizes power, kingly power. At the beginning of our journey, we were under the influence of Justice as a victim. Life was seen as fair or unfair, just or unjust. Now, having nearly completed the journey of the outer circle, we are learning how to act in harmony and in a just way with all creation, all animals and plants, all beings of Creation. We realize that Justice means "giving to every man his due" — and not only to every man, woman and child, but to every creature of God's creation. As you can appreciate, this is a very high level of being. A person at this stage has developed a certain command of life and Wisdom is now rendering him capable of dispensing Justice. The scepter symbolizes the ability of a highly evolved person to evoke respect and trust and take responsibility for large groups of people.

THE SYMBOLS ON THE INNER PATH OF DISCIPLESHIP

It becomes clear that, having moved all round the outer circle, a person is now living and acting under the influence of these five powers in a much more enlightened way. It may take many lifetimes for us to truly learn from all these experiences, but when we do, there comes a time when we want to enter the path of discipleship. The Buddha left the opportunity to become king in order to enter the path of discipleship and become enlightened. Jesus likewise rejected the offer to become an earthly king.

We no longer want to stay on the periphery of the circle, but, starting at the left leg, we begin to move along the lines of the Pentagram itself, rising directly up to Truth, then down to Justice, up and across to Love, back horizontally across to Wisdom, and back to Virtue, before finally entering the center itself. We are evolving into the body of Cosmic Man.

THE STAIRCASE AND THE DOOR

The first initiation, as we enter the inner part of the Pentagram, is represented by a picture on the **Left Leg** of a **Door reached by easy steps**. These are the easy steps of heightening one's commitment to goodness, deeper understanding and greater consciousness. One is now taking up one's destiny on this planet in a much more conscious way and playing one's part in the whole cycle of creation. We are increasing our understanding of what it means to live a virtuous life, and, in so doing, are moving towards the **Head**, Truth.

THE SPIRITUAL MASTER

At the **Head**, just under the word "God," we find the **Face of the Spiritual Master**, who will differ in name according to one's chosen path, but whom one might call the Cosmic Christ. We pass through the heart level on our way to Truth, and develop a heart connection with a great being (such as the Cosmic Christ) who will enable us to fully embody Truth.

This relationship with the Spiritual Master enables us to move from being merely peripheral participants of humanity, to becoming integral members of the body of Cosmic Man. I use the word, **Man,** coming from the Sanskrit **Manu** meaning "the thinking species," the thinking race, the thinking being, and I am reminded of St. Paul's description of **Cosmic Man** in Ephesians 4:

"a perfect man,...the measure of the stature of the fullness of Christ: that we,...speaking the truth in love, may grow up into him in all things, which is the head..."

THE STEEP AND STONY PATH AND NARROW DOOR

Having reached the **Head** of the Pentagram, we want to express Truth in all areas of life, all spheres of being. We move on to live out our experience of Truth on the path of Justice. We have risen from the **Left Leg**, and now go down to the **Right Leg**. As we have already experienced in **Square**, as Yarmila Mentzlova points out (in her excellent book in French, ***La PanEuRhythmie***, now out of print), the head and the two legs form the firm basis on which the human being stands and plays his or her part in creation.

At the point of Justice is the picture of the Steep and Stony Path and Narrow Door. This is the narrow door that Jesus spoke of in Matthew 7, ***"strait is the gate and narrow is the way that leads unto life."*** One approaches this door from a steep and stony way, which may mean going through a great deal of suffering. Those who have experienced great suffering, once they are able to forgive, are able to rise quickly to a much higher state of evolution. This fact goes some way towards helping us understand the positive role suffering can play in this world.

I see Mahatma Gandhi as a very good example of one who was totally dedicated to expressing Truth in the realm of Justice, as described in his autobiography, ***My Experiments with Truth.*** He became a lawyer, and his whole life was spent in search of true Justice. He brought justice into every detail of his relationships, both personal and public, and modeled this so fully that the world has been different ever since. A man like Gandhi is establishing the principle of Justice very firmly in his own life, as well as in the world. We know from studying Gandhi's life that this means severe self-discipline — symbolized by climbing a steep and stony path and passing through the narrow door — a much tougher initiation than the one at the point of Goodness leading towards Truth. This is the kind of suffering one takes on willingly, because it leads to Divine Love.

As Mother Teresa taught, *"Suffering is a great gift of God; those who accept it willingly, those who love deeply, those who offer themselves know its value."* We may go through some very unjust and difficult situations. One thinks of people like Solzhenitsyn, Mandela, and countless others who have willingly embraced great suffering and, in so doing, have been the means of generating great love in the world as a whole. This is not suffering that is karmicallly deserved. It is suffering that is taken on in the way that Jesus took on suffering, in order to dissolve something in the consciousness of humanity and open up the way for Love.

THE EYE

Once we reach the point of the ray of Love, we come to the **Eye** which leads us on to Wisdom. A person who is truly grounded in Love has the ability to see and to understand beyond the normal. That person has true insight into the events of the world and into other people's hearts, as do all true Spiritual teachers. That all-seeing **Eye** moves us toward Wisdom, because if you can truly see into the hearts of people, you won't judge by externals. You'll have the wisdom to understand the true inner evolution of people, and so be able to help them grow and evolve.

THE TREE OF LIFE

At the point of the ray of Wisdom we find a tree — the **Tree of Life**. All the truly great and wise Teachers of humanity are like a tree of Life, sustaining, nurturing, sheltering and healing all who come under their influence, both in their lifetime and beyond. The word "virtue" in Latin means "power." People at this stage of evolution have developed all virtue. They have an inner power which flows out in their lives as pure virtue, like Jesus whose touch or will could raise from the dead, bring total healing, or who, even when nailed to the cross, could say *"Father, forgive them!"* A person who is fully self-realized has a virtue, a power, which is totally healing and life-giving for all of humanity.

THE CENTER OF THE PENTAGRAM

As we move to the center of the Pentagram, we find several symbols. The two inter-twined snakes symbolize the duality of human existence, which has to be integrated and transcended. There is also a circle with a cross, and another circle beyond. These are so esoteric I prefer not to try and expound them further. At this point, a Soul is so fully in harmony with Divine Will that he has become one of the great guiding lights of mankind, possibly beyond incarnation, one of the pure beings guiding humanity from a higher level of being.

Perhaps we can glimpse now the amazing play of creation that we dance in the Pentagram.

"THE GREAT SCHOOL OF LIFE"

The three ancient Cyrillic letters at the top and bottom of the Pentagram stand for the Bulgarian words, "The Great School of Life." Around the outer circle of the Pentagram are words which remind us how we can best work within this great School: "In the fulfillment of the Will of God lies the power of the human Soul."

In fact, Peter Deunov said that the fastest way to evolve is to have

"a heart pure as a crystal,
a mind bright as the Sun,
a Soul vast as the Universe,
and a Spirit powerful as God,
and one with God."

Dancing the Pentagram in Montana

DANCING THE PENTAGRAM

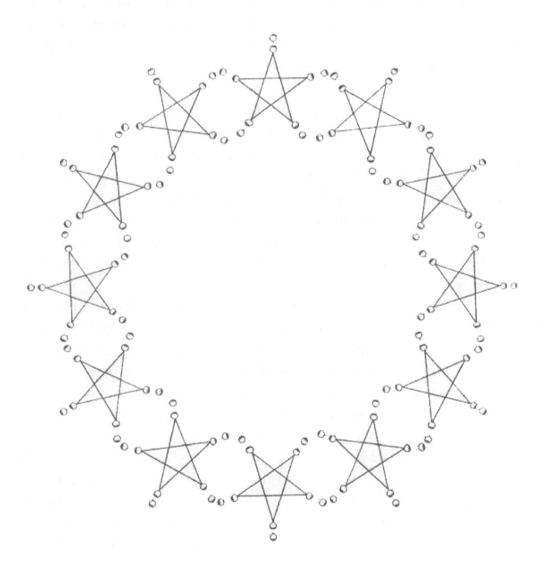

THE FIVE PRINCIPLES IN THE BODY OF COSMIC MAN

The Pentagram represents the body of Cosmic Man. The five points of the pentagram represent the **Head, Left Hand, Left Foot, Right Foot,** and **Right Hand** of the body. Each couple in the Pentagram, therefore, will represent in turn the **Head, Left Hand, Left Foot, Right Foot,** and **Right Hand** of the body of **Cosmic Man**, which correspond respectively to its five Principles: **Truth, Love, Goodness, Justice and Wisdom.**

Each human being is like a cell. Each of us is evolving, just as the cells in our bodies are evolving, and, as we evolve, we move through all the different aspects of what it is to become fully human. We learn to play our part as a cell in an arm or a leg, or as a brain cell, or as a specialized cell in the eye or the ear. In our own body, the individual cells are like human beings in a great cosmic entity, each playing their part in the good functioning and health of the whole. In the early stages of evolution, the cells are all the same. Then, as the body evolves, the cells begin to specialize and develop their own unique contribution to the whole.

The Music at the center of the circle represents the Central Sun, the Divine Source of all being, from which each "ray" is one of the twelve Divine powers emanating out from the Source, a representation of Cosmic Man. Ideally there will be twelve rays round the center. Each ray is going to unfold into a star, making twelve stars around the center.

We are becoming stars or jewels in the crown of the Creator.

The whole of humanity, Cosmic Man, is represented in one ray of creation, and that ray is going to turn around the Central Sun, unfold its full potential as a visible star, and then re-fold into an invisible ray. I like to use the word re-fold. The great American genius, Walter Russell, said that each of us unfolds into a human life and then re-folds back into our Source. When we move out of incarnation, we're re-folding, (becoming invisible on the physical plane,) and I feel that this is very well expressed in this dance of the Pentagram.

In the ancient traditions of India they say that whole cycles of creation happen in this way. A Ray goes out from the central Divine Source of creation and unfolds through millions and millions of years, creating universes, galaxies, races. All play their part and evolve, and then re-fold again into the invisible, unmanifest energy of the Godhead. It is this huge, gigantic cycle of creation that we play out in this dance.

For each pentagram there needs to be exactly five pairs, so the sixth pair will drop off and join other pentagrams dancing further out around the main inner twelve radiating from the center. We then all make a quarter turn to the right, to face counter-clockwise round the center, so that the partners are now one behind the other, instead of side by side.

THE PENTAGRAM'S FIVE DANCE SEQUENCES

The Pentagram is danced in five sequences, (all of which are then repeated five times as a whole.)

1. FORMING THE PENTAGRAM

Throughout the movements of the Pentagram except for the last, the arms are held horizontally out to each side, starting and ending with the hands pointing to each other, palms down, in front of the heart. The arms open out sideways in horizontal semi-circles each time the right foot steps forward.

When the music starts, we move forward with the right foot first, and take eight steps all together in a counter-clockwise movement around the music at the center of the circle. On the eighth step, the people in the two **Feet** (the second and fourth pairs) will bring their feet together and stay in place, just marking time with their arms. Meanwhile the other three pairs (the two **Hands** and the **Head**) will continue forward another eight steps. Then the **Hands** will stand still marking time, while the **Head** will go on another eight steps.

This represents symbolically what happens as our bodies evolve from conception. Cells in our hands evolve further than cells in our feet. Then the cells in our head evolve even further — to form our brain, eyes, and ears. At any given stage of evolution, some choose to stay and perform the function of feet, while others choose to evolve and perform the function of hands, and yet others move on to perform the function of head with its highly evolved and specialized cells performing intricate and delicate functions in the eyes, ears, brain, etc... We evolve the same way in the body of Cosmic Man.

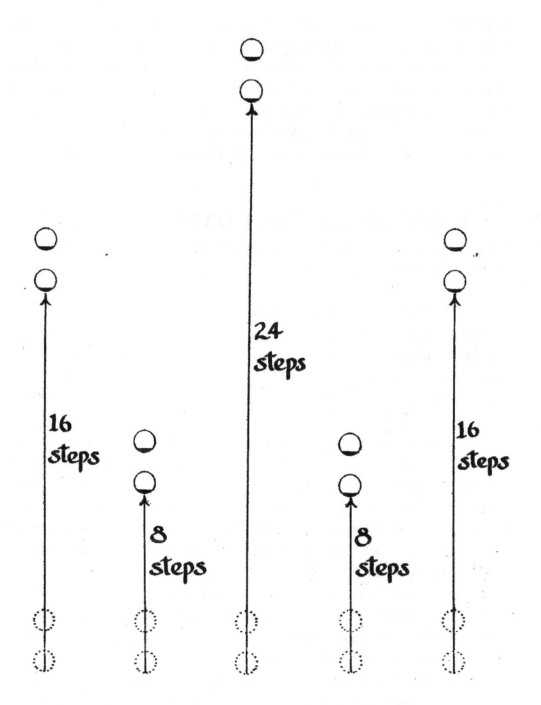

When we have each developed our own unique function, we all turn to face the center, for we now have to learn to function together as one organic whole. The pair forming the **Head** has to do the most turning; and isn't it true that the more evolved beings in society at any given time also have to display the most flexibility, if they are not to lose touch with the rest of humanity? The front partner in the pair turns 180 degrees to face the center, while the partner behind walks round in a semi-circle in order to stay behind. The **Hands** turn a little less far to face the center. The front partner will make a 120-degree turn, and the partner behind will walk 1/3rd of the way around the front partner to line up behind. (The front partner always stays in front, and the one behind is always the supportive one, the follower). The **Feet** do the least amount of turning; they turn 60 degrees or even less, and again the followers will line up behind the front partners.

This is a very beautiful moment in the dance, when we all turn to face each other and begin to feel the love and joy of all working and moving and being together as one great whole. We see the beauty and wholeness of what has been created and understand the importance of acting as one organic whole, a lesson that humanity is only just beginning to contemplate now! As we transition from hierarchical Piscean to egalitarian Aquarian thinking, we realize that we each have our own place and time in which to lead, and that, when we are in perfect star formation, it no longer matters to us personally what part we are playing. We are all radiating, facing each other, equidistant, in balanced partnership...

It is crucial to have a sense of this moving picture, before we practice the dance, because the learning of the Pentagram happens within the mind, rather than out on the field. This picture needs to be clear in our consciousness, in order to manage the dancing of it with precision and grace.

2. UNFOLDING THE PENTAGRAM (Part 1)

At this point, when the five pairs are facing the center, the music changes to a minor key, which is more inward, introspective. Having fully evolved in their present functions, each person, each cell, must now move on to learn to perform other functions in the body of **Cosmic Man**.

The sequence of movements through the Pentagram is the same as that described in the earlier section, **The Symbols on the Inner Path of the Disciple.** Simultaneously from all five pairs, first only the front partners move to the second position to the left. (The one from the **Left Foot** moves to the position of the **Head**, the one from the **Head** moves to the **Right Foot**, the front person from the **Right Foot** moves to the position of the **Left Hand**, the one at the **Left Hand** comes to the **Right Hand**, and the front person at the **Right Hand** comes to the **Left Foot**.)

In this part of the dance all move equal distances at the same moment, but in different directions, for we each tread our own unique path of discipleship.

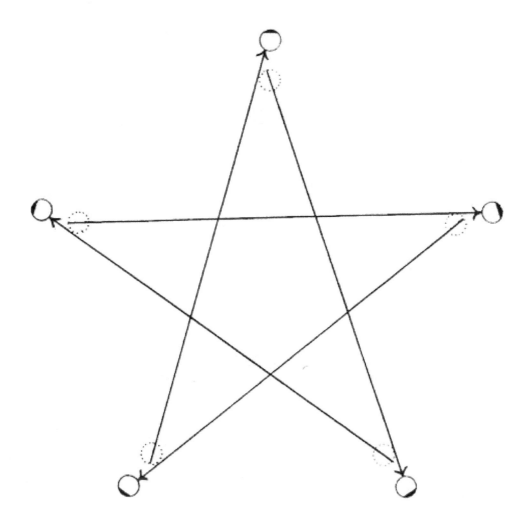

As the front partners move on to their new positions in the pentagram, the second partner of each pair moves forward two steps to make way for the new person to come behind him.

We have to stay very attentive to the Pentagram as a whole and our changing positions within it, and particularly remember where the **Head** is, so that we recognize it even with the new players there. This dance is a real exercise in holding the invisible pattern in our consciousness — not allowing ourselves to be distracted by changing appearances within the Divine play of Creation, but focusing on seeing and understanding the underlying pattern and perfect functioning of the Laws of the Universe.

3. UNFOLDING THE PENTAGRAM (Part 2)

We each have to have our connection with our partner very well established. We can see this particularly when we come to this next stage. We are all now paired up with a different partner, not our true partner. This is rather like what happens in the play of creation! We all have a soul mate or twin soul, but most of the time we're not with them. Yet, even though they're doing something else in the journey of creation, that connection between us is still known on a soul level, and so we are eventually drawn back together. In the next sequence of music, the second person of each partnership (now standing in front of a new temporary partner), will catch up with and take their place behind their original partner. The original partners are once again reunited, but in a new place in the body of **Cosmic Man**.

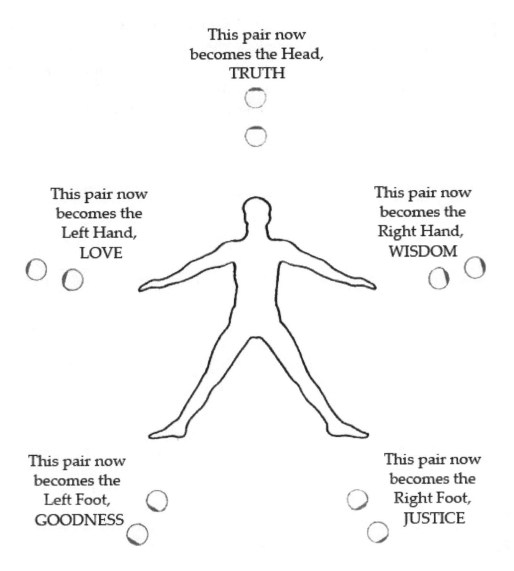

This pair now
becomes the Head,
TRUTH

This pair now
becomes the
Left Hand,
LOVE

This pair now
becomes the
Right Hand,
WISDOM

This pair now
becomes the
Left Foot,
GOODNESS

This pair now
becomes the
Right Foot,
JUSTICE

At this point we have to be very aware that we have left our previous place, and are now occupying a new position where the role is different. It is particularly essential to remember which couple are the **Head**, and relate throughout the sequence to them, because the **Head** has to lead.

In the story of evolution, what is crucial is not so much who we are, but what part we're playing. As people become more and more highly evolved, their ego gradually thins away and disappears, until all that matters is the task that they've been given and gladly undertaken. One no longer cares if nobody notices. The important thing is that the task gets done with love and to the best of one's ability.

A person is only a true member of Cosmic Man when they reach a level of transcending ego so that all their energy goes into playing their part to perfection, rather than worrying about whether others can see who I am and if I am getting the glory that's due to me. Some species, like ants and bees, are much better at this than human beings!

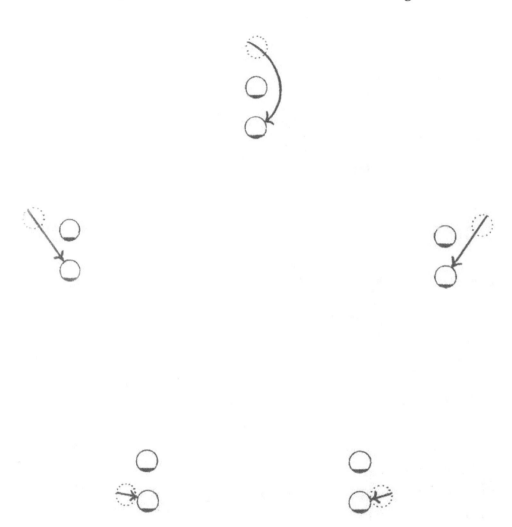

4. RE-FOLDING INTO A RAY

The next stage is the re-folding of the Pentagram. The five couples have been facing the center, and now they turn. The new **Head** (the couple who were previously the left foot) will make the greatest turn, 180 degrees. Always, the more we evolve, the greater our challenges and our need for flexibility and openness to the new Direction.

As the forward one turns 180 degrees in place, the follower will stay behind by walking in a semi-circle around the front partner. The two **Hands** will do a 120-degree turn and the two **Feet** will do a small 40-degree turn. All five pairs will now be facing toward the head, with the back partners all standing behind their front partners.

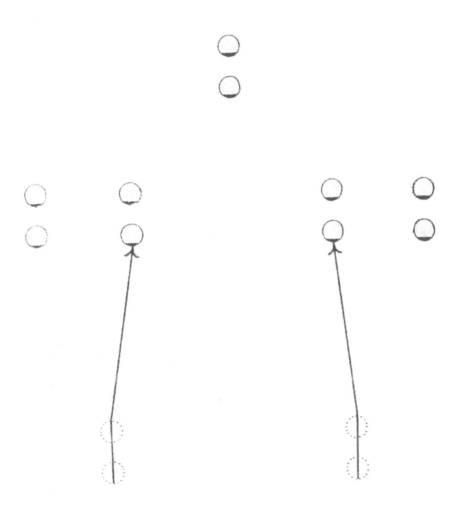

Again, the music changes and the **Feet** move up to take their positions between the two **Hands** and on each side of the **Head**. To accomplish this, the **Left Hand** and the **Head** stay in place, until the other three have lined up with them. (When practicing, it can be useful to have the **Head** raise their hands, so that they can be used as a point of reference for the others to position themselves.)

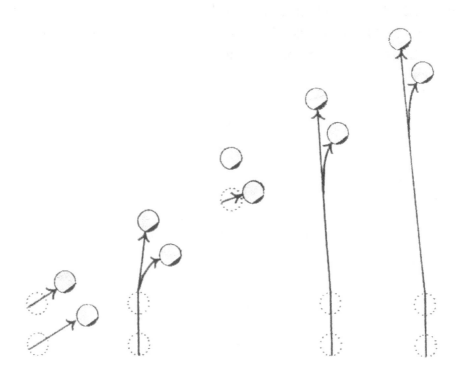

Once all are in a straight line (from the center of the circle through the **Left Hand, Left Foot, Head, Right Foot** to the **Right Hand**) we prepare to all turn together slowly round the center (like a hand of a clock but counter-clockwise) with the **Left Hand** taking very small steps to keep the connection with the center.

5. PROCESSING THE RAY

We have re-folded the Pentagram, and the Pentagram-stars have re-folded into Rays turning around the great Source of Creation. This is a triumphal moment and, as the music goes from a minor key to a major key, we enter a wonderfully joyful sequence, celebrating the completion of the cycle of Creation.

The arm movement changes for this final sequence. Our two hands start in front of our heart, thumbs touching, palms facing forward and fingers pointing up. They then move straight up together, as in a vertical breaststroke swimming motion, in front of our face and over our heads.

They then separate and move out sideways and down in two large semi-circles, before coming together again in front of the diaphragm and moving up again past the heart, palms facing forward throughout.

When all five pairs are abreast of each other, they will all move forward together, like a hand of a clock moving counter-clockwise, the ones near the center taking very small steps, so that the ones further out can keep up with them. As throughout the PanEuRhythmy, they are orienting themselves at all times to the center, where the Music comes from and which represents our Divine Source. Each individual Pentagram, "star" or ray is finding its true place in the whole cycle of Creation.

The music at the center of the great circle transmits the energy of the Divine, the energy of Creation. It is vital at all times to stay closely attuned to the Music, for this (and not the movements) is the heart and life-blood of the dance. The movements only serve to convey through our bodies and consciousness and all around us the healing and regenerating power of the Music, emanating as it does from a Divine Source.

THE FIVE CYCLES OF PENTAGRAMS

After this we repeat all five sequences five times, each time forming new pentagrams, with new people at the **Head**, **Hands** and **Feet**. In this way each one has the opportunity to dance from each perspective.

This is evolution. We have to come back for many lifetimes, so that we can become every part of the body of Cosmic Man, and learn Love, Truth, Wisdom, Justice, and Goodness. We have to really soak ourselves in these energies, until we have experienced every part of what it is to be a full human being. In the Cayce readings, it is very interesting to see how, through different lifetimes, people learn and work on different lessons, and how each person moves at their own pace, depending partly on their own inner desire and partly on the needs of their society.

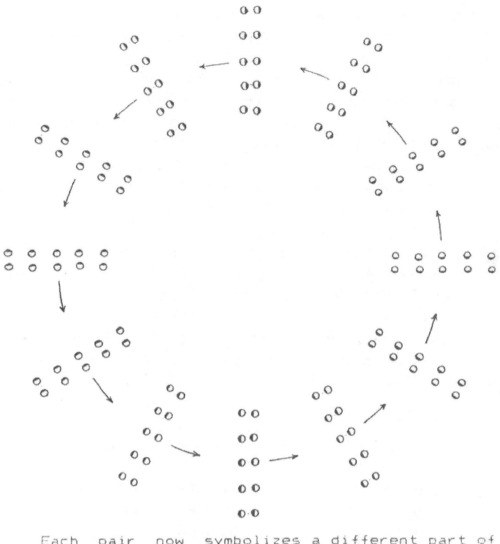

Each pair now symbolizes a different part of the Cosmic Man:

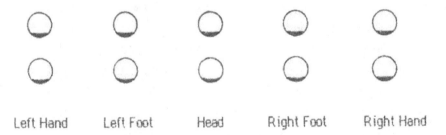

| Left Hand | Left Foot | Head | Right Foot | Right Hand |

Dancing the Pentagram in Montana

Description of Movements for the PENTAGRAM

For each pentagram there needs to be exactly five pairs, so the sixth pair will drop off and join other pentagrams dancing further out around the main inner twelve radiating from the center. We then all make a quarter turn to the right, to face counter-clockwise round the center, so that the partners are now one behind the other, instead of side by side. The five pairs in each pentagram will form a double row radiating out from the center (which will be to their Left through most of the dance.)

The music is majestic and triumphal. The **Pentagram** is played through five times, so everyone gets to dance in each of the five positions: head, left and right hands, left and right feet. For most of the dance (through **Re-folding into a Ray**) the arm movements remain in the same **horizontal** plane. The palms of the hands then turn to face forwards and move out and back in a **vertical** plane, when the music becomes bolder and brighter for **Processing the Ray** in the last 16 bars of the dance (which are a repeat of the first 16 bars.)

Throughout the dance, as the dancers step forward, they need to remain mindful of their connection with the center and not move away at tangents. This means curving their forward movements slightly to the left, in order to keep at the same distance from the center throughout each individual pentagram.

1. FORMING THE PENTAGRAM: (16 bars)

Starting position: The five pairs form two rows, partners one behind the other, feet together, hands in front of the heart, elbows out to the sides horizontally, palms down.

Bar 1: See **Diagram page 242:** Right foot steps forward and hands swing out to the sides in a **HORIZONTAL** plane, palms facing down throughout. Left foot steps forward and hands sweep back in a **HORIZONTAL** plane to the starting position. (Diagrams 1a/b opposite)

Bars 2-4: As in bar 1. On the last step of bar 4 the two pairs (2nd and 4th) forming the **Feet** of the Pentagram bring their feet together and stay in place for the next 12 bars, continuing only the arm movements.

Bars 5-8: The other three pairs (1st, 3rd and 5th) continue forward (in lines curving slightly to the left around the center) for another 8 steps. On the 8th step the feet come together, except for the **Head** pair.

Bars 9-12: The pair forming the **Head** continue on forward for another 8 steps (in a line curving slightly to the left around the center.)

Bars 13-16: See **Diagram page 243:** In the next 8 steps the pair forming the **Head** turn round to face the others behind them, Right shoulders now towards the center. The front partner slowly turns round 180 degrees in place, whilst the back partner makes a semi-circle, staying behind the front partner. The other pairs also adjust their relative positions, so as to form a five-sided figure, all facing in towards one another, partners one behind the other.

2. UNFOLDING THE PENTAGRAM (Part 1) (8 bars)

See **Diagram page 245:** The **front** partner of each pair moves forward (past the first pair on the left to the second pair on the left) and goes to stand behind the remaining partner of the **second** pair on the left, who moves forward two small steps to become a temporary front partner.

3. UNFOLDING THE PENTAGRAM (Part 2) (8 bars)

See **Diagram page 246:** The second partner then goes to join the first partner, who takes two small steps forward to again become the front partner. In these two parts, each partner accomplishes one unique stage in the **Inner Path of Discipleship (Left Foot** to **Head** to **Right Foot** to **Left Hand** to **Right Hand.)**

1a

Pentagram   *1b*

2

4. RE-FOLDING INTO A RAY (8 bars)

A: See <u>**Diagram page 248:**</u> The five partners all turn to face in the original counter-clockwise direction of the Dance, (their Left shoulders towards the center,) as follows:
The **Head** turns 180 degrees round to face in the opposite direction,
The **Left Foot** turns to the Left to face forward, (36 degrees approx.)
The **Right Foot** turns to the Right to face forward, (36 degrees approx.)
The **Left Hand** makes more than a quarter-turn to the Left to face forward, (108 degrees approx)
The **Right Hand** makes more than a quarter-turn to the Right to face forward, (108 degrees approx.)

B: See **Diagrams pages 249 and 250:** The five partners now start lining up again in a straight line, as follows:
The **Head** and **Left Hand** mark time until the others catch up.
The **Right and Left Feet** advance to between the Hands.
The **Feet** and the **Right Hand** then move forward on a radius from the **Left Hand** until lined up with the **Head** in the middle.

5. PROCESSING THE RAY (16 bars)

See <u>**Diagram page 252**</u>: Left shoulders towards the center, all are now in a double straight line radiating out from the center. As we process forward, we turn our palms to face forward and describe **VERTICAL** semi-circles with our hands sweeping up and out, then back up and round and down to the heart again. (See **diagram 2**, previous page.)

The music is a repeat of the first 16 bars. All march triumphally forward together, swinging the arms out and back in **VERTICAL** semi-circles, and singing. All need to keep the whole line in mind, so that the outer dancers can comfortably keep up with the inner ones. In practice the Left Hand virtually marks time in place, keeping the connection with the center, which is crucial. In the last bar our left foot joins our right foot, and our arms come to rest by the sides of our body.

THE FIVE CYCLES OF PENTAGRAMS

Between each of the times we dance the **Pentagram**, we pause, then repeat the sequence, starting in our new positions in the pentagram.

After dancing the **Pentagram** five times in all, we turn to greet and acknowledge our partner and all the other dancers in our pentagram.

In Bulgaria a formal verbal greeting is exchanged. In some countries we embrace each other.

~ Summary ~

Forming the Pentagram		− all walk forward − Feet stop − Hands stop − Head stops; all turn to face centre	8 steps 8 steps 8 steps 8 steps	MAJOR THEME
Unfolding the Pentagram	(i)	− first member of each pair crosses to point 2nd on his/her left	16 steps	MINOR THEME
	(ii)	− second member of each pair crosses to join his/her partner	16 steps	MINOR THEME

Head → R.Foot → L.Hand → R.Hand → L.Foot → Head

If you have difficulty in working out your new identity, concentrate on remembering the original orientation of the Cosmic Man *on the ground* − it is only you that moves during stages 2 and 3, not the Cosmic Man.

Re-forming the Sunbeam	− all pairs turn to face forwards, taking their bearings from the Head; Feet walk forward into line with Hands	8 steps	MINOR THEME
	− Left Hand and Head stay in position while everyone else gets in line	8 steps	
Processing the Sunbeam	− Stay in line! Be aware of the geometry of the Sunbeam and sympathetic to the striding ability of those at the edge.	32 steps	MAJOR THEME

257

Peter Deunov

The gentle, kindly touch of Peter Deunov's eyes, and the soul-full, joy-filled swing of his music have steadily reached into my being over the years and warmed my heart with his loving presence. Sometimes it was as if a gentle breeze were wafting me along, and at other times he has made his presence known through others.

On occasion, when I have been teaching PanEuRhythmy or talking about Peter Deunov, people have seen him near, or sensed his presence, vibration, or colors. On one bleak winter morning when I was feeling sad and discouraged, my phone rang and a bright voice said, "How are you? Peter Deunov told me to call you." When I later met this remarkable woman in person, she told me that she had for the previous three days been hearing his voice saying, "Call Ardella! Call Ardella!" and finally she had.

That was the start of a most remarkable year for me, teaching PanEuRhythmy not only in California and all over the USA, but also in Australia, New Zealand and even in Brazil, as well as taking a group of Americans for the first time to the annual PanEuRhythmy camp in the Rila Mountains of Bulgaria. Sitting there by the spot where he used to pitch his tent and listening to the sheer beauty and loving soulfulness of his music being played by musicians who, as children, had lived in the community which had grown up around him, I was moved to tears by the love and joy he had brought into the world.

I remembered how, when still living in England, I had been taken to this region during the era of Communist oppression when nobody dared dance the PanEuRhythmy openly, and we quickly, quietly, and wearily made our way up the mountains, past the Seven Sacred Lakes, only to reach the summit in the fog. Finally, in answer to my desperate prayer, the fog had cleared — just for a few brief seconds, but long enough for me to take the last two photos I had been saving for the view from the top — a memory which would carry me through the next ten years.

Now, ten years later, I could sit here once again, openly this time and in the sunshine. This time, after four years of teaching, I had brought a group from the U.S.A. with me, and we were surrounded by close to one thousand people gathered from all over the world to experience these sacred places where he had taught just over half a century ago. And now Maria Mitovska also shared with me how PanEuRhythmy was born, as she had heard it from several of those who were close to the Master Peter Deunov.

In the early years, when Peter Deunov used to take the disciples camping in the Rila mountains, they used to sleep out under the stars around a big bonfire and get up in the very early hours to climb to the top of a high mountain in order to see the sunrise. Everyone loved being in the Master's company and looked forward to these opportunities, arduous though they might be.

One day Peter Deunov asked a trusted disciple, Metodi Shivarov, to rise very early the following morning and climb alone to the top of Mount Mussala to be there before dawn. ("Mussala" means "close to God" and is the highest of the Rila mountains.) Earlier that day all the others had gone with Peter Deunov to see the sunrise from the top of Mussala, and Metodi had volunteered to stay behind to tend the fire and take care of everyone's belongings, so Peter Deunov was rewarding him for his selfless spiritual service by giving him a special assignment.

Very early the following morning Metodi rose and set out in the dark to find the path to the summit. On the way, he seemed to be aware of a light guiding him in the dark. He continued for several hours until he reached the top, where he sat in darkness waiting for the dawn. Almost imperceptibly the darkness paled, and light began to appear on the Eastern horizon. Metodi sat and watched…

Gradually he became aware of beings of light moving in the growing luminosity. He was entranced, and even more so when he began hearing delicate sounds of music, and started noticing that the beings of light seemed to be dancing to the music… Like a celestial symphony the music became louder and more expressively beautiful, while the beings of light grew in numbers and danced ever more ecstatically.

At last the music rose to a great crescendo as the direct rays of the sun started shooting out from beyond the distant horizon, and the beings of light scattered across the sky. The music then gradually died away as the full orb of the sun emerged over the horizon.

Metodi stayed for a while absorbing deeply this amazing experience, the music still ringing in his ears and his whole being radiant with the energy of the music and dancing he had just witnessed. He had seen other sunrises from Mussala, but never one like this! Finally he made his way back down the mountain to the camp where Peter Deunov sat smiling and waiting for him.

While others gathered around, Peter Deunov quietly asked him to share his experience, then smiled and said: "Yes. you have seen right. And one day I will be teaching you all to take part in that dance." This was the sign he had been waiting for. The time had come for humanity to be given the opportunity to dance in harmony with the dance of all the beings of light in Creation.

In a later talk on PanEuRhythmy, quoted in **The Wellspring of Good – The Last Words of the Master Peter Deunov**, he said:

"The Evolved Beings above also dance PanEuRhythmy. They make similar movements; and if our movements are in accord with theirs, then we will make contact with them and will receive their blessing. In order to make this contact, it is not only necessary that our PanEuRhythmic movements be correct and rhythmic, but that harmony exists between the mind, heart and will of the performer; that is to say, the performer should have Love, Purity and an enlightened condition of the spirit.

"PanEuRhythmy, the way it exists above, cannot be done here on earth because humankind is not ready for it. We are given as much as is possible and in the most accessible form."

Yes, PanEuRhythmy is truly an opportunity to engage with the beings of Light and Love and Joy from the Divine world, and enter into communion with one's own soul and the Soul of the Cosmos. It is so simple to take part in, yet needs long-term work to master truly.

Peter Deunov was born on 12 July, 1864, according to the Western calendar, (on June 29, 1864, St Peter's Day, according to the Julian calendar current at the time in Bulgaria). [See www.sophiafoundation.org or: www.paneurhythmy.org for the very interesting article by Robert Powell *"Peter Deunov's horoscope: The superior conjunction of Venus with the Sun"*]

Peter Deunov's father, Konstantin Deunovsky, was a priest in the Bulgarian Orthodox Church. It is said that as a young man, he made his way to Mount Athos in Northern Greece, just south of Bulgaria, thinking his calling was to become a monk. In a church in Thessaloniki he was met by an old priest who told him that his path was a different one and that he should marry, as one of his children would have a very sacred mission to fulfill. They talked of the approaching end of the five centuries of Turkish oppression in Bulgaria and the new opportunities for the Church, and he gave him a sacred relic, over which Bulgarian priests had been praying for a hundred years for independence and Christian unity.

"Konstantin Deunovski 1830 - 1918 Activist for national, educational and religious freedom in Ustovo and Varna."
(Inscription on statue in town square of Ustuvo, Bulgaria, near his church.)

Konstantin returned home and became a priest in the Bulgarian Orthodox Church. In 1856 he married Dobra, the daughter of the pioneering schoolmaster he had been working under and with whom he had a profound spiritual affinity. They had two sons and a daughter, Maria. As a priest, Konstantin was innovative, dedicated, and visionary. He worked tirelessly for the liberation of his people from the Turks, and at Mass he broke with tradition by reading the Gospel in Bulgarian instead of in Greek. There is a story that later his youngest son, Peter, once asked his father about "what I gave you in the church at that time."

Peter was of a deeply spiritual nature, and could often read people's minds and predict the future. His friends and family soon learned to pay careful attention to what he told them. He insisted on learning the violin, against the protests of those around him who said this would not help him earn a livelihood. All his life his violin was his constant companion, and he could often be heard even in the small hours of the night playing gently as a soft prayer wafting heavenwards. He was constantly improvising and composing, and later his followers learned to write down his songs to preserve them for posterity.

Dobra died while Peter was still very young, but all his life he remained very close to his father and sister, Maria. As he grew up, he lived for a while in Varna on the Black Sea with Maria who had married a Methodist minister — a fact of special interest to me as my own parents were Methodist ministers in West Africa and Haiti. It was while with them that he became profoundly impressed by the life and practical Christianity of John Wesley, and started at the American Methodist School.

He also worked for a while as a village schoolmaster and was successful in persuading the parents of his pupils to give a better example to their aggressive children by giving up their own intolerant attitudes and making peace with one another. Then, in 1888, he set sail for the United States to study at Drew Methodist Seminary in Madison, New Jersey. His thirst for knowledge was so great that he also took the opportunity to study many other subjects, including science and medicine there and at Boston University. He earned his living doing simple work like carrying luggage for passengers from the harbor, and cheerfully accepted whatever people wanted to give him, affirming always that "God will provide!" Once having saved enough money to buy himself some new clothes, he stopped to talk with a beggar, then invited him to his place and finished up giving him food and his new clothes.

The people who knew him there spoke of him with awe. He loved to take them on excursions in the countryside and talk to them of the beauty and secrets of Nature and the laws and wonders of the Universe. They also loved to hear him playing his violin. At times he would be found alone deep in meditation, from which he would "awake" as from a deep and beautiful dream.

One fellow Bulgarian, Grablashev, told of how Peter Deunov once  invited him to accompany him into the forest. They came to a beautiful lake and a boat took them across to an island in the middle. There a group was solemnly gathered waiting for him, and the twelve of them entered a large hall and sat around a long table. Grablashev had been told not to ask questions or to record any of the proceedings, so this meeting remains a mystery. Some days later Grablashev attempted to retrace their steps, but was totally unable to find any lake in that area"

Peter Deunov in his youth

On his return to Bulgaria in 1895, Peter Deunov wrote his first book, *Science and Education,* and was offered many posts in the Methodist and Orthodox Churches as well as in the Theosophical Society, but he always refused to accept a salary, and the authorities could not accommodate such an unconventional arrangement. He had transcended the narrow limitations of any established orthodoxy, for he was entering into initiation for his life's work. Instead he spent some years in comparative seclusion — studying, writing, and often in the mountains in deep prayer and meditation. In 1898 at the age of 33, he and his father together had a vision of the Christ blessing and consecrating him. From then on he received intensive guidance on his future work of sowing the seeds of a new Culture of Love, and he adopted the Spiritual name, Beinsa Douno.

In 1898 he issued a "Call to my People" and in 1900 an invitation to the first annual Convention. When the only three who turned up asked where all the others were, Peter Deunov replied, "Now you are only three people, but you will become thousands.... The hall is not empty. The chairs are occupied by invisible beings." By the end of his lifetime there were about 40,000 people following his teachings.

I am reminded of how, when the Maharishi Mahesh Yogi first came to London, they hired a large concert hall and issued many invitations. When no one turned up, he insisted nevertheless on giving his full talk, saying that the hall was full of invisible beings and one day would be filled with visible human beings — a prediction which was fulfilled over and over again in his years of popularizing meditation in the West.

I often remember this when I am invited to teach PanEuRhythmy and very few people turn up. As Jesus said, "If you have faith, even as a grain of mustard seed, nothing will be impossible for you." (Matt 17:20) If the seed is sown on fertile soil, it matters not how few come, the seed may multiply a hundred-fold, as I have often experienced.

In the first few years of the twentieth century, Peter Deunov traveled round the country extensively, giving illuminating scientific lectures and studying the Bulgarian people carefully. As well as being a musician, violinist, and composer of a very high order, he was skilled in medicine, healing, and phrenology, and accounts of his often miraculous healings abound. People gathered around him to learn from his wisdom and be renewed by his love.

At the 1912 Convention he first gave out his **Testament of the Color Rays of Light**. This esoteric book coordinates the color rays of Light with the seven Spirits of God through key texts from the Bible for use in healing and Spiritual growth.

From 1917-18 Peter Deunov lived in Varna, where he met and started training the young **Mikhael Aivanhov**, who later took the teachings to the West, when Bulgaria was closed off by Communism. (See Omraam Mikhael Aivanhov's account of his experiences as a devoted disciple in his own

Mikhael Aivanhov in his youth

words in "Aupres du Maitre Peter Deunov." Prosveta.com) Thanks to Aivanhov who later was recognized by great Masters in India as a true Master and was given the sacred title of Omraam, this great Spiritual tradition continues to inspire countless souls all over the world.

The Hall at the Izgrev Community

By 1905 a couple in Sofia, the capital, had invited Peter Deunov to share their small home, and here people would gather at 5 am before going to work to hear his early morning lectures. When there were too many to fit in the house, he would speak from the open window, and people would sit or stand in the yard, even in freezing snow in winter.

In 1922 Peter Deunov started a Spiritual School which he continued for 22 years until the end of his life in 1944, and over 4,000 talks were given, most of which were recorded in short-hand and later transcribed. There were two esoteric classes, one for unmarried young people and the other for adults. In addition, there was a lecture on Sunday mornings open to the general public, and many came from far and near to hear him, to question and ponder his answers. Discipline in the esoteric classes was very strict, but self-imposed. Before the start of class the students would gather in silence, while musicians softly played some of his music and songs. This would set the tone for his teaching. This powerful method of attunement enabled him to dispense with the rigorous tests traditionally imposed on would-be students in ancient Mystery Schools, for his Spiritual music would raise the consciousness of those present to be able to understand his message. Music therefore played an essential and integral part in his teaching methods.

Nature was also central in his teachings, for he maintained that modern man, by considering Nature to be mechanical and insensible, had lost his connection with the Divine and become estranged from himself. The PanEuRhythmy therefore was given as a way for people to attune to Nature through movement and music, thereby re-connecting with their own Soul and with the Divine world.

Peter Deunov always encouraged people to attune to nature and spend as much time as possible out of doors, particularly in the early hours of the day, when the sunlight discharges the greatest spiritual healing and revitalizing energy and quickens the spirit. The day starts by experiencing the radiance of the dawn before sunrise, for it is at this time that the spiritual energies enter our atmosphere most profoundly.

Lunch in front of the Hall at Izgrev

Peter Deunov himself would always take a walk in the dawn hour, and soon others started coming to join him, for he said that at this time the Divine world is most accessible to us. Still today, and certainly in the

Peter Ganev

Rila mountain summer camp, people contemplate the dawn for half an hour or more until sunrise when they rise and raise their right hands to receive the first rays of the sun. [Care is, of course, always taken to avoid damage to the eyes from gazing directly at the sun for too long once it has risen above the horizon.] They then join in songs of Divine contemplation and joy.

To the East of Sofia there was an open hillside where Peter Deunov liked to take his dawn walks, and many would join him. Soon they started calling the area "**Izgrev**" (meaning "Sunrise") since it was here that they would gather for the sunrise meditation and exercises. In 1926 the August Convention was held here in the open, with many people camping around. Afterwards a group of them built a lecture hall there.

The Hall had many windows for the sunlight, a library and above it a small room where Peter Deunov lived very simply. From this room people would often hear sweet strains of music from his violin, even in the very early hours of the morning, long before the time for the lecture at 5 am. Gradually, people began to buy land and build homes and gardens around, and so the community of Izgrev arose.

Living in the Izgrev Community was an important aspect of work in the spiritual school. Here the principles of the Teaching would come alive, as people learned to apply them in their everyday communal life. Under the daily influence of their beloved Master they sought to live in harmony with Nature and one another, and considered it a Spiritual privilege to help one another. They continued their jobs in Sofia, tithing their income and each supporting in whatever way they could. They built their own homes, each planting their own garden and orchard, and there was also a communal garden. Two of our leading musicians today, **Yoana Strateva** and **Peter Ganev**, grew up as children in this

Community and, along with others, are now working to fulfill Peter Deunov's prediction of a New Izgrev. (The original Izgrev was demolished by the Communist regime in 1954, to make way for a Russian Embassy in that location.)

Yoana Strateva

The annual conventions continued and grew in strength and power. At first they had been held in Turnovo, then in the 1920s, 30s and 40s in Sofia. Whenever possible they were held in the high Rila mountains, when the snow melted in July and August. Peter Deunov maintained that, in order to truly connect with our Soul and Spirit, it is important to rise beyond the astral vibrations of civilization by going at least once a year up into the mountains above the tree-line. People of all ages would accompany him, because they saw in him a true embodiment of his teachings, and would also join him in sleeping out under the stars, even though the weather was often challenging.

A visitor to the Rila camp, Rev. Metodi Markov, once commented:

"If today we could speak of saintliness, Deunov is a saint. He is also a Magi, in the sense that this word has been used in the East, a truly wise man and a profound mystic!

"Deunov is yet to be appreciated as a preacher, a pastor, and a priest, as a hiker and as a Bulgarian, as a speaker, a teacher, a theologian and a sociologist; as a psychologist, an ethicist and a philosopher; as a prophet, an organizer, a vegetarian, a teetotaler, a healer, a scientist, a believer, a musicologist and a patron of the arts. He has been involved in all these activities and has brought them to fruition."

The two favorite regions for the summer mountain camps were near the highest mountain of all, Moussalla (meaning "close to God") and among the Seven Sacred Lakes of Rila, where the PanEuRhythmy is still danced each summer by large numbers of people who gather from all over the world. Peter Deunov would introduce the movements in Sofia, then all would gather to dance them in the Rila mountain summer camp.

Each year from the early 1930s a few more movements were given, until finally the **Sunbeams** were added just after the outbreak of World War 2. The glorious message of hope and the ultimate triumph of good over evil sounding in the following words of the **Pentagram**, (written shortly before by a close disciple, Peter Pamporov,) must surely have revived the sinking spirits of many during the darkest period of the century:

> *"Here we come, beaming bright,*
> *Royal bearers of Light!*
> *From the heights we descend,*
> *Help to Earth we would lend.*
> *Will you hear our friendly call today?*
> *We bring Love and Freedom,*
> *With the Truth clear your way."*

The whole **PanEuRhythmy**, together with the **Sunbeams** and **Pentagram**, were finally performed in the mountains with Peter Deunov in 1942. After he passed away on December 27, 1944, his faithful disciples were sorely tried under the very repressive Communist regime, and everything went underground for forty-five years. The books were burned or buried in secret places, people's activities were closely scrutinized by the secret police and many were arrested, imprisoned or disappeared.

It was towards the end of these forty-five years that I first had the privilege of learning the **PanEuRhythmy** and connecting with those brave souls who were still continuing to practice and keep it alive until the day when it would at last be able to come out again into the open — when the iron hand of the KGB was finally released by Glasnost in 1989. Those visits in secret during the years of harsh oppression and danger are very precious to me, for it was then that I got to know the ones who were close to the Master and who are now no longer with us. Their Light and Joy and Wisdom will ever be in my soul, and I am particularly thankful to **Brother Boris Nikolov** (generally regarded as the father of the movement after Peter Deunov's passing) for giving me his blessing to bring **PanEuRhythmy** to the USA. I am also grateful for the rigorous training I received from Brother **Kroum Vazharov** with **Maria Mitovska** — giving me the confidence of learning the precision of the movements. Kroum and Boris were very close to Peter Deunov for

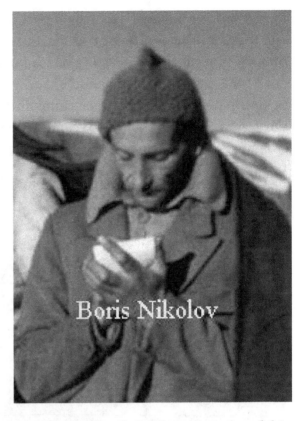

Boris Nikolov

over twenty years, and were key members of the inner circle of his esoteric school.

Peter Deunov himself would usually take part in the **PanEuRhythmy**, leading from within the circle, while the orchestra played at the center, or sometimes he would watch from the outside. He would encourage people to let the **PanEuRhythmy** engage their full attention, for in this way the benefits are manifested most fully. The music, singing, movements, and inner meaning can each more than occupy one's full consciousness, so there is never any room for boredom. On the contrary, the more **PanEuRhythmy** is practiced, the fuller and deeper the experience and the energy gained for the whole of the day.

From the first day of Spring until the Fall Equinox, the Sunrise meditation is followed by **PanEuRhythmy** — as much as one has time and inclination for. On Sundays and special occasions and certainly in the Rila mountains, the **PanEuRhythmy** is danced all the way through, followed by the **Sunbeams** and the **Pentagram**. For those who wish, there are also other exercises done without music — the seven Sunrise breathing and meditative Exercises, and a series of twenty-two Health

Exercises for rejuvenation of each part of the physical and subtle bodies. All these practices are best done out of doors and provide excellent opportunities for re-energizing oneself in communion with Nature.

At this point I would like to share with you excerpts from an account of life in the annual summer camp in the Rila Mountains of Bulgaria, written by Stephen Bonn who came with us in 1996:

PanEuRhythmy near the Fifth Lake and the tents of the Rila Mountain Camp in the far distance above the Second Lake

"My Bulgarian Pilgrimage:

"Going into the Rila Mountain region was like stepping back in time. Riding through the plains approaching the mountains, in an old Russian car, we passed people on the roadside with horse-drawn wagons. At the base of the trail leading to the Seven Lakes, we dropped off our heavy luggage for porters with horses to take up to camp. Later, we saw goatherds with their goats in the mountains. This closeness to the earth was deeply impressive.

"Waiting for our guide to come down from the Seven Lakes, we met an interesting couple from France, who spoke English and were waiting to go with us to the same campsite. They are followers of Omraam

Mikael Aivanhov. Many people were converging on this base camp. A busload of Russians arrived. We met an older but sturdy Bulgarian woman, who would be carrying all of her provisions on her back.

"Our guides arrived, and we started up the trail. During the three-hour journey we passed through various landscapes as we increased our elevation. Initially, the trees were tall, and there were areas with numerous raspberries and blueberries. Eventually, at higher elevations, we got to a landscape of shrubs and low trees. At a rest stop, a guide pointed out the Sleeping Giant Mountain in the distance, so named for its resemblance to a sleeping man. Legend has it that Orpheus defeated a giant that is now sleeping as this mountain, and that one should be careful not to 'wake the giant.'

"The Rila Mountains were a site for Orpheus and his mystery school, which makes them anciently sacred. According to Master Beinsa Douno (the spiritual name adopted by Master Peter Deunov) these are one of three major mountain sites of esoteric initiation in the world, the other two being the Himalayas and the Alps. The Rila Mountains are very ancient and are supposed to be the only mountain range which was never under water. High invisible beings are said to live in these mountains, who can bless those who visit here with the proper reverence

Sayings and symbols given by Peter Deunov inscribed on the Rock Spring where (behind the woman) the water gushes out through the marble hands by the third of the Seven Sacred Lakes of Rila.

"We eventually passed the First Lake, and soon afterward, our trail became steep and rocky. After we passed this more challenging portion, we arrived at the first of the campgrounds of the White Brotherhood. [This centuries-old term for the advanced Souls guiding humanity is often transliterated today as "Fellowship of Light."] Eventually, we reached our campsite, and were happily greeted by our Bulgarian hosts.

"Life in camp was rugged but wondrous. Our campsite was near the top of a hill in the mountains, between the Second Lake and the Lake of Purity. Our hosts had done a marvelous job of preparing the campsite with tents, a kitchen area, and a primitive latrine. Water was to be fetched from the sacred spring at the base of the hill between the Second and Third Lakes. This spring has water pouring out of marble "hands" that were carved by disciples of the Master. Various sacred symbols are carved in the surrounding rock. A large boulder that appears to rest precariously on a small base near the spring is the subject of one of the many stories about the Master. Although he generally preferred not to make a show of his powers, at least once he pointed to this boulder and made it rock back and forth. I believe that after hearing this story, I tried to push the boulder and it wouldn't budge. A flat rock that is painted with a spiral symbol is a place to stand on and make a wish. The Master said that carrying the water up to camp from the spring purifies one's astral body. All this spring magic is great motivation for engaging in this hard work.

"Before the break of dawn, we would gather at various high places with eastern views, to greet the sunrise. As the sun peeked over the horizon or through the low-lying clouds, we raised our right hands in communion with it and sang sacred songs from the Master, in Bulgarian. This was followed by prayers and readings, then breakfast — a perfect way to start the day.

"In the mornings, we went to various sites to dance the PanEu-Rhythmy with the Brotherhood. The sites are situated near various of the lakes. Maria Mitovska, one of our hosts, was my first partner, a graceful dancer, and she had various excellent tips for how to better perform the dance. Various musicians were at the center of the circle, playing violin, guitar, and other instruments. The circle grew larger as we approached

Meeting the Sunrise at the Rila Mount of Prayer

the climax of the gathering, which is August 19th, eventually forming two, possibly three circles. The inner circles were reserved for those dressed in white. The landscape added much magic to these dances.

One day, we danced in a fog and light drizzle, and could barely see the people on the opposite side of the circle. On other days, we were surrounded by majestic peaks in bright clear sky, and truly felt embraced by sacred blessings.

"We often went on expeditions in the afternoon, visiting various sites in the surrounding mountains. On one expedition, we were led up a steep cliff, then up a trail, and down to the Sixth Lake. This lake has a crystalline quality about it, which was enhanced by a large ridge of snow that remained near its edge. We were serenaded along the way by one of the PanEuRhythmy violin players, who would stroll ahead of us with seeming ease as we struggled along.

"I got severe knee pain on the way down from the above-mentioned expedition. A doctor in the Brotherhood applied a poultice of roasted onions coated with olive oil to my right knee that night, a remedy from the Master. The next day, my knee was much better, and finally, after learning to walk without jarring my heel, the problem had almost gone.

"On the final expedition, we went past the Seventh Lake, and onwards to the highest of the nearby peaks. To explain the lake formations in this region, there are two major groupings of lakes. One is a grouping of seven lakes, with two small lakes to the side. The seven lakes are said to carry the energies of the seven major chakras. The two side lakes are called the Lake of Purity and the Lake of Contemplation, and can be felt to carry the energies corresponding to their names. Near the peak of the high mountain, we were afforded a view of another system of lakes, which were in a landscape of round hills and valleys, colored in a light bluish green. They have a very harmonious quality. Specifically, the Master has spoken of them carrying a feminine magnetic quality about them. Perhaps, in another trip, we will have a chance to absorb this energy by walking through this region. For now, we absorb some of their energy, simply through the beautiful sight of them.

"In the evenings, there were concerts held next to the site where the Master used to camp. We heard a beautiful solo performance by a professional tenor, who sang both classical pieces such as Schubert's Ave

Maria, and spiritual songs of the Master. Those who know them also sing along with various of these spiritual songs. Concerts were also given sometimes by the PanEuRhythmy musicians, immediately after PanEuRhythmy. Music is a key part of the whole experience here. The "Rila Word Sheet" Ardella provided contained the words to a number of the songs, so we were able to join in on these occasions. Other songs were simple enough to quickly learn and sing along with. I hope to get access to more of this music before my next trip. It can be quite moving."

(**Stephen Bonn, California**)

The Master giving a talk on the Mount of Prayer after Sunrise
Vessela Nestorova behind the Master and Boris Nicolov taking notes

Speaking of the cosmic significance of the PanEuRhythmy, the **Master Peter Deunov** said:

"Paneurhythmy is a vast science which in the future will be studied and its knowledge fully applied in implementing the Laws of the Universe, and protecting peace and harmony in human souls. For this purpose I have placed in your hands this, the key to my Teaching. If you dance the Paneurhythmy correctly, the positive forces of Nature will flow through you and connect you with one another, and connect all of you with the unbounded Cosmic Circle of Great Beings."

Like all true and great spiritual Masters, Peter Deunov never made any special claims for himself. He attributed all to the Divine world, and spoke of himself as a servant and mediator of the Divine gifts of healing, teaching, music, and the PanEuRhythmy which came through him. And it is certainly true, in my experience, that PanEuRhythmy is a transmitter of Divine energy, healing, creativity, and joy. It softens and awakens the heart, and makes possible in our lives whatever is the next step in our evolution. Again and again I have experienced people making breakthroughs in their lives with PanEuRhythmy, which had not previously been possible. As one man recently put it, "The next step had been waiting for me for ten years, but I had not been able to see it until my mind was cleared through the PanEuRhythmy." Another man experienced a major breakthrough in his relationship with his family which twenty-five years of workshops, seminars, and courses had not previously made possible.

I have known some people have significant past-life recalls, while others experience real healing, both physical and emotional, through the PanEuRhythmy. Some develop new abilities and most people's creativity and awareness is heightened. Many people are moved to tears by the deep love and joy they feel and cannot quite understand. For each person, the gift and experience are unique, and improve with wholehearted practice, study, and dedication.

As Peter Dawkins, the spiritual teacher and founder of the Francis Bacon Research Trust in England wrote:

"The PanEuRhythmy movements are profound
in both their effects and their meanings,
and learning to become proficient in their practice
and to understand them
is something that will probably be endless.
It is one of the most worthwhile "yogas" for the Western
man that we have ever come across...
and can relate man in a purely harmonious way
with other people and with the whole of nature.
It is a great force for brotherhood and peace in the world,
and it needs widespread use and study
both to do it justice and to make use of what is
undoubtedly
a great gift to mankind."

The Master Peter Deunov

"How PanEuRhythmy changed my life"

I was introduced to Paneurhythmy
after coming to the USA from my native Bulgaria in 1991.
By "chance" I met the late Ernestina Staleva,
a disciple of the Enlightened Teacher Peter Deunov,
whose spiritual name was Beinsa Douno.
This meeting turned my life around.
Before that, I had felt alone on this far-away continent,
but thanks to her, I found my Paneurhythmy family.
Erna loved very much the Paneurhythmic exercises,
having learnt them at Izgrev,
the settlement founded by Peter Deunov's followers.
She would share them with love and joy
like a candle igniting many more candles,
and I am thankful to be one of those candles.
I will not forget the day when she told me,
"Tomorrow it is you leading the group, I will not be there."
I was petrified, as I had never danced on my own.
I remember I wrote on my hand the names of the exercises
in case I forgot which one came after which.
We found a beautiful place for Paneurhythmy —
Mount Pollux in Amherst, with its 360-degree view.
Sometimes we also danced among the flowers
in Erna's beautiful garden.
Her house was always a welcoming home for visitors,
as she shared her wisdom, her stories related to the Master,
and her simple delicious meals.
I joined Erna also in translating, publishing,
and distributing the words of the Master.
For a couple of years my work took me to the West Coast.
This was not an easy time, as I missed my East Coast friends,
but, looking back, I realize that my few years in California
were really the most beneficial time for my spiritual growth.
Before that, there was separation and animosity between
Paneurhythmy groups on the East and West Coasts,
mostly over details in some of Paneurhythmic movements.
While living in the San Francisco area,
I came into contact with the groups there
and found wonderful and dedicated people.

By performing the exercises with them
and coming to know them in person, I found that
the exactness of the physical movement is not so important,
but what matters is the harmony and peace
these mindful spiritual exercises bring.
As a result of these unpleasant, though beneficial lessons,
I finally understood properly the Master's words,
and we now work together and in harmony
as true followers of the path of Love and Light.
Paneurhythmy has become a part of my life.
Even during the week before going to work,
I would try to find time to practice..
On days when I had done Paneurhythmy,
my colleagues would tell me they could see a difference in my
interactions with them and in my work-related performance.
Often I would use my break around 10 am to go outside
and do part of the Paneurhythmy exercises.
I will not forget September 11th 2001.
I was planning to go outside as usual at 10 am.
However, around 8:30 am I got an urge
as if a voice was nudging me, "Go outside, dance!"
Finally I went to my place in the garden.
Somehow I was dancing with full concentration,
every movement was full of prayer and
my hands were sending waves of energy of Love and Peace.
I continued sending silent prayers as I returned to work.
Then I heard the news about the attack.
I am convinced that
when we dance Paneurhythmy with concentration
we help not only ourselves, but the entire world.
People who read auras tell me that after Paneurhythmy
my aura becomes lighter and brighter.
So, let us dance Paneurhythmy in Love and harmony,
united with all mindful and enlightened beings!

Antoaneta Krushevska — *Amherst, January 12. 2012*
(Translator, editor and publisher of Peter Deunov's teachings.)

How PanEuRhythmy evolved

Peter Deunov had been waiting for the right moment to start introducing PanEuRhythmy, (see account on page 260.) Boris Nicolov*,

one of his most devoted disciples, tells how one Spring day in the 1920's the Master and some of the close disciples were out in Nature practicing folk songs and dances, when the Master started singing a melody and then suggested expressing it in movement. After a while he himself gracefully, naturally and rhythmically began dancing to the music, and the first

Boyan Boev with the Master

movement of PanEuRhythmy was born. From then on he could often be heard creating further movements on his violin in his room at night, and the following morning he would try out the new exercises with the group. He was focused and inspired and his face would glow with an inner fire. His creative power grew stronger and stronger, and the PanEuRhythmy exercises then arose one after another.

Peter Deunov would first demonstrate the PanEuRhythmy exercises to a group of "sisters" in the brotherhood, and then entrust them with teaching these movements to all the others. Some of the main people involved in working on the PanEuRhythmy with the Master in the early days were Boris Nicolov, his wife Maria Todorova, Boyan Boev, Eleena Andreeva, Pasha Todorova and Savka, who acted as his stenographers, Kroum Vazharov (from 1927) and other disciples. They were joined by Milka Periclieva, (when she moved to Sofia from Varna in 1933) and Katya Griva (after she came to the Master in 1932.)

Elena Andreeva

* See www.paneurhythmy.org and go to <u>Information</u> then <u>History</u> for accounts by Brother Boris Nicolov and others on the beginnings of PanEuRhythmy.

Katya Griva singing

In the mid-1930's a small book was published in Bulgarian, giving only the text of the PanEuRhythmy lyrics (composed mainly by Olga Slavcheva under Peter Deunov's inspiration.) Peter Deunov then asked Milka Periclieva to describe the movements in writing, which she did in consultation with Boyan Boev, and in 1938 the Brotherhood published in Bulgarian a guide-book to PanEuRhythmy and the Pentagram, (titled simply: "Beinsa Douno: PanEuRhythmy,") giving Milka's descriptions of all the movements, together with the spiritual meanings and music by Peter Deunov.

Unfortunately, as newcomers learned the movements through personal exposure, none of the early books described these in sufficient detail. For example, the 1938 book loosely describes the switch between right and left arms in **Opening**: "These movements are repeated until the 19th bar, after which the arms change over, the right hand staying on the hip and the left moving in front of the chest, out and in. These movements continue to the end of the music." Thus it remains unclear how to

Milka Pereclieva

coordinate the arm movements with one's footsteps here, and it is impossible to know exactly what was the original teaching and practice.

In 1941 another book, *The Master Beinsa Douno: Paneurhythmia, Songs of the Harmonious Movements*, was published, containing the music by Peter Deunov and the underlying principles*** of the PanEu-Rhythmy, together with all the lyrics (for the 28 movements by Olga

*** For the <u>Seven Principles underlying PanEuRhythmy</u>, (which need deeper study than is possible here,) see www.paneurhythmy.us <u>About PanEuRhythmy</u>

Slavcheva and Peter Deunov and for the Pentagram by Peter Pamporov), but it had no descriptions of the movements.

Vessela had become one of the closest disciples of Peter Deunov, after she returned from her studies in the United States as a young woman, and it was she who did most of the earlier translations into English. Some of us had the great joy of knowing her before she passed away in 2002. (See Barnaby Brown's Introduction to the Music and Lyrics, p 160.)

The first book on the Sunbeams was published in 1942, *Sunbeams: Music, Movements and Words of the Master,* with music by Peter Deunov, lyrics composed by Vessela Nestorova, and descriptions of the movements of the Sunbeams as well as their spiritual meanings.

As his following increased, the Master had said that if children throughout Bulgaria could learn PanEuRhythmy, it would change the fate of the nation for the better. He finally asked Milka Periclieva and later Vessela Nestorova (who were both teachers) to introduce PanEuRhythmy in the schools, and together they started working with the school-teachers. They continued together until 1943, when the first bombs were dropped on Sofia and the Master said that this work would have to be postponed till a more favorable time.

Bulgarian music often has an odd number of beats in a bar (e.g. 7/8), so Bulgarians are accustomed to uneven rhythms in music. Variations have arisen in different places and between different musicians and experts on PanEuRhythmy as to whether there should be 40 or 41 bars in the music for movements 7, 8, 9, (**Opening, Liberation, Clapping**). In the 1938 book these three movements are described in a way that fits into 40 bars of music, although the written music had 41 bars. In addition, the arm and foot movements are described without enough details, giving rise to alternative ways of dancing, differing in whether the left hand in **Opening** and **Clapping** are coordinated with stepping on the left or the right foot.

During Peter Deunov's lifetime, one of the disciples, harpist Assen Arnaoudov, highly praised by Vessela Nestorova and very influential among the musicians, met together with a group of disciples to discuss the discrepancies in **Opening, Liberation** and **Clapping**. They decided to experiment with deleting one bar of the music (either the 19th or the 30th bar), so that the music would fit the movements as Peter Deunov had approved them. This brought the music to the more traditional even number of bars and accommodated the description of the dances given in the 1938 book on PanEuRhythmy. However, the majority of musicians continued to play the 41-bar version and in recent years the Bulgarian Brotherhood, more accustomed to odd numbers, voted to keep

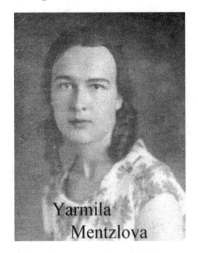

Yarmila Mentzlova

the 41 bars, while in other countries the 40-bar version had become more established.

Yarmila Mentzlova, a professional dancer and choreographer and a student of Isadora Duncan, had been singled out by the Master as the most natural and accurate interpreter of the PanEuRhythmy. He had seen that she was able to dance it accurately the very first time she heard the music, without having been shown the movements, so much so that he commented to the disciples, "Look what correspondences there are between the music and the movements!" After Peter Deunov's passing, around 1947 Maria Todorova, Elena Andreeva and others realized that explanations of the

movements in the 1938 book were not detailed enough to prevent different interpretations among those who would rely solely on them to learn the dance. So they invited Yarmila to work with them and together they produced a more precise description of the movements which still retained the 41 bars in **Opening, Liberation** and **Clapping**.

They also took photos and made several copies of Maria Todorova demonstrating the movements with Yarmila. However, they too omitted information about how to coordinate the arm and leg movements. For example, in the

Maria Todorova and Yarmila Mentzlova

descriptions of the movements for **Opening,** their manuscript reads: "At the end of bar 19 the left hand is placed in front of the chest and the right on the right hip. From bar 20 the movements are performed with the left arm, and the right hand remains on the right hip to the end of bar 41."

Yarmila was a very gentle and sensitively gracious person, beloved by all who knew her, especially in Paris, where she was working when the Communists took over Bulgaria shortly after World War 2 and the country was closed off from the West. In the 1940's she had married Kroum Vazharov, but the situation in Bulgaria was too difficult for her professionally and, as she was of Czech origin, she was finally able to leave. Most of her later life she taught in France. There, true to her assignment by Peter Deunov to use her talents as a professional dancer and choreographer, she produced in French her own professional book with extremely precise and detailed descriptions of the movements, *La Paneurythmie: Le psychisme humain en Union avec l'Harmonie Universelle (PanEuRhythmy: the human psyche in Union with Universal Harmony),* based on the 1938 book but with Assen's version of the music. Yarmila's book was published in France by Yarmila's friends shortly after her death from an accident in 1984. This was the standard and only non-Bulgarian text in the years when I was studying PanEuRhythmy intensively. I still find it unsurpassed and have a profound regard for Yarmila both personally and professionally, as do all those who knew her personally.

The 1938 book, being the only one actually approved by Peter Deunov during his life-time, has always been highly regarded, and many, like Yarmila Mentzlova and Viola Bowman, have continued to feel it important to stay as close as possible to that version. Viola Bowman, (who together with Ernestina Staleva first introduced PanEuRhythmy in the northeastern United States,) in her book, *Pan-Eu-Rhythmy — Exchange of energy between Man and Nature,* incorporates Milka Periclieva's descriptions of the movements from the 1938 book. Likewise the first book in Spanish, *Paneuritmia – Manifestacion Ritmica del Divino Principio Cosmico de Creacion,* (by Aida Kurteff, the wife of Jorge Kurteff, an early disciple of the Master who emigrated to Argentina,) is basically a translation of Yarmila Mentzlova's book and therefore also follows the 1938 book.

Throughout the Communist regime it had not been possible to publish the manuscript drawn up by the four "sisters" in 1947, but finally this century it was published as ***Beinsa Douno: Paneurhythmy.*** In 2004 this version was officially adopted by the Bulgarian Brotherhood and a further phrase was added:

"From bar 20 the left arm opens as the left leg steps forward while the right hand remains on the right hip to the end of bar 41."

It is, of course, essential to respect the meditative, life-giving spirit of PanEuRhythmy, and dance in harmony with whatever group one finds oneself with, as did as all these above-mentioned teachers of PanEuRhythmy. On one's own, however, one is free to dance in whichever rhythm feels most conducive to true harmony with one's spirit and with Nature. As Peter Deunov himself said in his talk on PanEuRhythmy in ***The Wellspring of Good,***

> *"The Evolved Beings above also dance PanEuRhythmy.*
> *They make similar movements;*
> *and if our movements are in accord with theirs,*
> *we will make contact with them*
> *and will receive their blessing.*
> *In order to make this contact, it is not only necessary*
> *that our PanEuRhythmy movements be correct and rhythmic,*
> *but that harmony exists*
> *between the mind, heart and will of the performer;*
> *that is to say, the performer should have Love, Purity*
> *and an enlightened condition of the spirit.*
> *"PanEuRhythmy, the way it exists above,*
> *cannot be done here on earth,*
> *because humankind is not ready for it;*
> *we are given as much as is possible*
> *and in the most accessible form...*
> *"A special school for the study of the PanEuRhythmic*
> *movements and songs is needed."*

Appendix: Details of some of the variations in the movements.

A: According to the books on PanEuRhythmy published by Maria Periclieva and Boyan Boev in 1938, by Viola Jordanoff Bowman in 1979, by Yarmila Mentzlova in 1983, and by Kroum Vazharov and Maria Mitovska in 1993 —

In Opening: As the right foot steps forward, the left arm swings out to the left, and the right hand moves from the heart to the right hip. As the left foot steps forward, the left hand returns to the heart.

In Liberating: The arms swing out as the right foot steps forward, (in accordance with Peter Deunov's teaching about the creative and constructive principles, as well as Classical Chinese teaching, where we learn that energy moves out through the right side and in through the left.)

In **The Sun is Rising: In "Zoun mezoun"** the arms open forward from the heart as the right foot steps forward.

B: According to the book on PanEuRhythmy published posthumously in 2004 and based on descriptions of the movements in the manuscript drawn up during the Communist period by the "four sisters" Maria Todorova, Elena Andreeva, Yarmila Mentzlova and Katya Griva:—

In Opening: As the right foot steps forward, the left hand moves up to the heart, and the right hand drops down to the right hip. As the left foot steps forward, the left hand moves out to the left.

In Liberating: The arms swing out as the Left foot steps forward.

In **The Sun is Rising: In "Zoun mezoun"** the fingers come to the heart as the right foot steps forward.

All the above authors knew Peter Deunov personally.
The following authors (who were born too late to meet him in person) leave the above choices open: —

David Lorimer: *The Circle of Sacred Dance* in 1991
Ardella Nathanael: *Dance of the Soul* in 2012

USA Heartland in Harmony Gathering

**PanEuRhythmy participants and Ardella in Poland
with Lidia Klimowicz and Arleta in front**

*"PanEuRhythmy workshops led by Ardella
are a wonderful time for everybody -
a period of real spiritual evolution.
These incredible workshops,
led with art, engagement and love
bring enthusiasm for PanEuRhythmy into our lives.
In PanEuRhythmy we find a new source of pleasure
and discover a new way of connecting with Nature.*

Ardella is an excellent teacher,
who can simultaneously lead workshops
for a whole group of people
and for each person individually.
The sensitivity, empathy and at once professionality
of this spiritually great, delicate, tiny woman
have the effect of making PanEuRhythmy
simple and understandable, easy and pleasant.
But the most important thing is that
PanEuRhythmy has become important and useful in our lives.
We experienced teaching with great power and peace.
Each new gesture released joy and opened our hearts.
We became acquainted with a philosophy of life
in harmony with Nature and with all around us,
and felt the need to open our hearts
and fill them with all goodness
and share it with other people.
It is a great joy to join in Ardella Nathanael's workshops,
who doesn't mind travelling long distances to come here
and share all the wealth of wisdom about PanEuRhythmy."

— Halina Wilcynska, PanEuRhythmy teacher in Poznan,
Poland: September 2007

Halina Wilcynska listening
to Peter Ganev in Poland

Ardella Nathanael

Ardella Nathanael is a true global citizen. Raised in West Africa and the Caribbean by British and French parents, Ardella was educated at the Universities of London, Cambridge, Heidelberg, and in Paris, graduating with an Honors degree in French and German, and later with a Social Work Studies Diploma from the London School of Economics.

For nearly a decade, Ardella Nathanael lived and worked in London as a teacher, social worker, and counselor to inner-city families. Fluent in English, French, and German, she taught these languages at all levels and acted as a simultaneous translator for the World Council of Churches and the World Student Christian Federation in Austria, England, France, Sweden and Germany. She is now learning Spanish...

Since her youth, Ardella Nathanael has been a student of the world's spiritual traditions and dance. Ardella has studied many forms of dance, including classical ballet, folk dance, Sufi dancing and Kathak Kali dance. She coordinated personal enrichment and meditation classes in London and taught meditation for the British Meditation Society for five years. Her group continued for eleven years until she left for the USA.

Ardella has been a student of PanEuRhythmy since 1983. She braved the Communist regime to learn PanEuRhythmy at secret meetings in Bulgaria started by founder, Peter Deunov. In 1986, she helped introduce PanEuRhythmy in Europe and Great Britain where she sponsored two teachers from Bulgaria to come and teach PanEuRhythmy.

Ardella Nathanael has been presenting PanEuRhythmy worldwide since 1988. She has introduced thousands of people of all ages to this powerful "Dance of the Soul." She has lectured and taught PanEuRhythmy in Great Britain, Europe, Poland, the United States, Australia, New Zealand, Costa Rica, Brazil, Colombia, Ecuador and Chile. Throughout the world groups of grateful students continue to enjoy the PanEuRhythmy, inspired by her teaching, encouragement and years of dedicated work.

Ardella's books, **Dance of the Soul** and **The Butterfly Dance,** continue to stimulate further interest in PanEuRhythmy and delight people in many parts of the world. Her charmingly illustrated children's book, **The Butterfly Dance**, introduces in story-form the idea of personal transformation and self-realization through PanEuRhythmy. Both books are available in English, Spanish and Polish, and can be ordered through her webpages at: www.paneurhythmy.us/Ardella.shtml

Ardella can be contacted at: 415-499-8027
Jeannette Prandi Way, Cottage 404,
San Rafael, CA 94903-1135, USA
ardella222@gmail.com

TO ORDER:
www.paneurhythmy.us
(and click on link: "Learn PanEuRhythmy with Ardella Nathanael")
www.everabooks.com
"Dance of the Soul" www.infinitypublishing.com
"The Butterfly Dance" www.createspace.com/3428947
"The Butterfly Dance coloring book" www.createspace.com/3428955
www.amazon.com

OTHER USEFUL WEBSITES:
www.paneurhythmy.org
www.esotericpublishing.com

"A true revelation"

"The first PanEuRhythmy workshop I attended
was for me a true revelation.
I had been trying to learn it
for a few months with a small group.
Unexpectedly, in those two workshop weekends,
the symbolism of the movements,
the history of the creation of the dance,
its connection with the spiritual –
all opened for me a new inner space.
The experience of dancing the PanEuRhythmy was a real joy!
In addition, the dance itself produced
an immediate physical well being
and, at times an "altered state of consciousness".
We use the arms a lot, activating the upper chakras,
and often after dancing with people hitherto unknown
we experience at the end a feeling of kinship.
I learned in that workshop that "PanEuRhythmy is a mirror,"
and that each of the twenty-eight movements expresses
a divine quality that we potentially all have and can develop.
The difficulties present in the actual execution
of any specific movement
go well beyond the physical level:
they can relate to the emotional, mental or spiritual
content of that exercise.
Thus, as we work on improving the movement,
connecting with the meaning as well as singing,
we are also working on ourselves —
in the nicest way in the world! —
uplifting our state of consciousness,
and deepening our spirituality.
In my work as a psychotherapist,
I sometimes teach a patient a movement
related to their specific issue, and improvements always ensue.
At other times I imagine a person in need
participating in our PanEuRhythmy circle,
and after a few days I invariably discover that this person
has benefited from their "participation," even without knowing it!

The music is beautiful.
It has a quality that penetrates deeply into our hearts
and induces the movements,
which seem to be born naturally out of it.
Dancing the PanEuRhythmy is an experience
that generates inner joy,
a feeling of communion with Nature
and with other human beings.
It opens us simultaneously to our own inner nature,
producing a meditative state, and to sharing with our partner,
with the circle of dancers and with all of humanity —
because of the irradiation of the ideas
contained in the movements.
To be in touch with the deepest part of our being -
dancing and singing among trees, birds and butterflies —
what more could one want?
PanEuRhythmy is a spiritual path, a physical discipline,
and above all a joy!
Among the many people I would like to thank
I will just mention three:
Maria Rosa and Glaucia who taught me the first steps,
and Ardella, the inspired teacher of that workshop."

Maria Eugenia da Rocha Nogueira, PanEuRhythmy teacher in Sao Paulo, Brazil.

Table of Photos
Photos can be viewed in COLOR in E-book version.
Page:

Index

CPSIA information can be obtained
at www.ICGtesting.com
Printed in the USA
FSHW011727171019
63063FS